DANI'S STORY

Diane and Bernie Lierow are parents to six children, including Dani, as well as foster parents. Their story won a Pulitzer Prize for the St P~ Times and was featured on Op live on a farm in ' miniature horses, goats, chickens, and Great Pyrenees dogs. Kay West is a veteran journalist and the author of three books.

Dani's Story

A Journey from Neglect to Love

Diane & Bernie Lierow
and Kay West

PENGUIN BOOKS

For Dani and William

PENGUIN BOOKS

Published by the Penguin Group
Penguin Books Ltd, 80 Strand, London WC2R 0RL, England
Penguin Group (USA) Inc., 375 Hudson Street, New York, New York 10014, USA
Penguin Group (Canada), 90 Eglinton Avenue East, Suite 700, Toronto, Ontario,
Canada M4P 2Y3 (a division of Pearson Penguin Canada Inc.)
Penguin Ireland, 25 St Stephen's Green, Dublin 2, Ireland (a division of Penguin Books Ltd)
Penguin Group (Australia), 250 Camberwell Road, Camberwell, Victoria 3124, Australia
(a division of Pearson Australia Group Pty Ltd)
Penguin Books India Pvt Ltd, 11 Community Centre, Panchsheel Park,
New Delhi – 110 017, India
Penguin Group (NZ), 67 Apollo Drive, Rosedale, Auckland 0632, New Zealand
(a division of Pearson New Zealand Ltd)
Penguin Books (South Africa) (Pty) Ltd, 24 Sturdee Avenue, Rosebank, Johannesburg 2196, South Africa

Penguin Books Ltd, Registered Offices: 80 Strand, London WC2R 0RL, England

www.penguin.com

First published in the USA by John Wiley & Sons 2011
First published in Great Britain by Penguin Books 2011
1

Photo credits: Pages 122, 128, 177, 190, 200 and 212 courtesy of Melissa Lyttle/
St Petersburg Times/Zuma Press. Page 264 courtesy of Empower Me Day Camp.
All other photos are from the Lierow family collection.

Printed in England by Clays Ltd, St Ives plc

ISBN: 978-0-718-15828-6

www.greenpenguin.co.uk

MIX
Paper from
responsible sources
FSC
www.fsc.org
FSC™ C018179

Penguin Books is committed to a sustainable
future for our business, our readers and our
planet. This book is made from paper certified
by the Forest Stewardship Council.

Contents

Introduction

Five minutes before the arrival of the school bus that carries my children over three miles of rolling, winding, narrow two-lane road, I walk with a posse of excited, yelping dogs from our ninety-year-old Tennessee farmhouse down the long drive to the gate at the end. The bus lumbers to a stop, the door wheezes open, and there is our twelve-year-old daughter, Dani, ready to deboard. Very briefly, she considers the steps, but quick as a blink she instead slides down the smooth steel hand rail on her bottom. I grab her up in a hug as she reaches the ground, she smiles, and after her older brother William latches the gate behind us, we walk together back to the house, navigating a path through the dozens of chickens that assemble in the pecked-bare ground outside their coop like pigeons on a piazza in Italy.

Dani opens the back door, drops her backpack on the floor in the mud room, and pats the inside dogs on their heads. She smiles when William's parrot squawks a greeting, and after a quick pit stop in the bathroom, she goes to the kitchen to refuel after a long day of lessons and classrooms. As the cat weaves its way between her legs, Dani opens the refrigerator door and contemplates the contents but

1

doesn't see anything that interests her, so she grabs a package of peanut butter crackers from the pantry. She chooses a plastic cup from the cupboard, swivels to the sink, turns on the tap, and fills the cup with water. Then she sits down at the table and digs into her snack. It is an after-school ritual being performed at that moment in that sequence in millions of households across America.

After the kids' snack, we go to the barn to check on our ever-reproducing herd of goats. While William and I begin the ritual of setting out food and clean water for the goats in the yard, Dani goes inside the barn to check on the new mamas and their babies in the area that serves as the nursery.

Once those chores are done, we go back to the house so the kids can settle down with homework at the kitchen counter while I start dinner. When Bernie comes home from work, he ruffles William's hair, tickles Dani till she squeals, and then takes a quick shower before we all sit down to eat. After dinner, if it's still light outside, Bernie likes to run around with the kids in the yard—he's an overgrown kid himself—and hike out to the back pasture to check on our four miniature horses. Baths, pajamas, bedtime stories, prayers, goodnight kisses, lights out, and the kids are finally in bed. Bernie and I collapse on the sofa in the family room, catch up with each other, watch the news if we can stay awake that long, and take one last peek in on William and Dani before calling it another very long day. The next morning, the alarm goes off at 5 a.m. and we start all over again.

It is totally routine and absolutely ordinary.

Yet in our family, even the routine is unpredictable, the ordinary is extraordinary, and the most mundane tasks are milestone achievements for our pretty, brown-eyed, blond pony-tailed, long-limbed daughter.

When Bernie and I first met Dani in the profound needs classroom of an elementary school in Land O' Lakes, Florida, she had just turned eight years old. She drooled, her tongue stuck out one side of her mouth, her head lolled to one side, she wore a diaper, and she drank—sort of—from a sippy cup tied to the leg of a table so that when she dropped or threw the cup, it would not roll away. She bit her own arms and hands, pulled at her hair, and hit the sides of her head with her balled-up fists. She did not make eye contact, engage with others, or like to be touched; she did not smile, laugh, or talk. She did have a repertoire of pretty impressive noises: a sustained guttural moan, a higher-pitched wail, an occasional piercing shriek, and a yelping repetitive "woo woo woo woo" that sounded so much like a European ambulance it made Bernie remark that in an emergency, she could be her own siren.

She had been in foster care since being discharged from Tampa General Hospital some fifteen months earlier, where she had spent four weeks after being removed from the rundown shack where she lived with her mother and two grown stepbrothers. She had been confined day and night like an animal in a tiny, filthy, dark room, alone and naked except for her diaper, uncovered on a cockroach-infested, soiled bare mattress. She was intermittently fed solid food from a can and was infrequently bathed, but she was never held, never kissed, never talked, read, or sung to, and never played with. She was never taken outside to feel the sunlight on her face. At nearly seven years old, she had never been taken to a doctor, had never been immunized, had never seen a dentist, and had never been to school. She was covered with thousands of bug bites, her arms looked like sticks, her ribs were clearly visible under pale skin, and her scalp crawled with lice under her matted and dirty hair.

Yet that day in the classroom, Bernie and I didn't know any of this. All we knew was that we had been so powerfully drawn to this little girl, whom we had seen only in her photograph in a gallery of children available for adoption, that we could not get her out of our minds. We had been told by the agency that we should do ourselves a favor and choose another child. Her primary social worker had strongly suggested that before we went any further, we see the movie *Nell* starring Jodie Foster as a "wild child" who was discovered living in the backwoods of North Carolina. She spoke a language no one could understand and lashed out at anyone who tried to come close to her. We watched it with William and one of our older sons, Paul. At one point, as we all sat transfixed by the story, Paul turned to us and asked, "Are you nuts?" When the movie was over, Bernie and I looked at each other and, as we so often do, read each other's thoughts.

We both knew we had to meet this little girl whose image had already embedded itself in our hearts, minds, and souls. The connection we felt with her before we even met her was so powerful that we never questioned it. It was as if we already knew her, and although we didn't know what lay ahead, we had no choice but to follow whatever or whoever was leading us to her.

As crazy as it sounded, somewhere in the back of our minds Bernie and I believed that if this inexplicable, mysterious calling was so undeniable, maybe she had been waiting for us all along.

1

Planting the Seed

The first time I brought up adoption to Bernie was about three years after we got married. We were still living in Tennessee, renovating a huge old house we had felt compelled to buy, working days at our jobs and nights and weekends on our home. I didn't have a specific child in mind or even a gender or an age. I was just testing the waters. Bernie's response was not exactly enthusiastic, so I put it in the back of my mind.

The next time I brought it up was after we moved to Florida and were living in our first house there. Our youngest, Willie, was not in school yet, and Paul and Steven still lived with us. Yet we were down to only three kids from five, and the thought had worked its way forward in my head enough for me to bring it up to Bernie again. I think I just casually mentioned it, kind of like, "How was your day, what do you want for dinner, can you take Steven to get a new pair of board shorts later, have you thought any more about adopting a child?"

As best as I can recall, his answers were, "Good. I can grill something. Okay. No."

So I dropped it again. Although Bernie had been an equal partner in adopting stray dogs and rundown houses, a child required quite a bit more than a pat on the head and a fresh coat of paint.

For as long as I can remember, adoption was something I felt that I was called to do. As an only child, I longed for siblings and a big boisterous family like the ones I saw on television. When I was born, my parents were quite a bit older than most parents of that day; my father was in his early fifties and my mom was forty-two. I was their fourth child, but the previous three did not survive infancy. I never knew that until later, and even then, it was not a subject either of my parents talked about. I know I asked them about having a brother or a sister and that they had looked into adopting, but in that era, they were considered too old.

I can't fathom the pain my mother had suffered when one baby after another died. Losing one baby would be a tragedy, but three? It's unimaginable to me. I've been known to cry for days over losing a baby goat. Maybe she became so worn down by her grief that she couldn't allow herself to feel anymore or become attached to a child when three had been taken away from her. Our relationship was always distant and cold. My mother was not in the least affectionate, and I longed for her to hug me, rub my back, stroke my hair. She took care of all of my standard needs—food, shelter, clothing, medical care, education—but she could never bring herself to tell or show me that she loved me. My father was different. I was his little girl, and I spent as much time with him as I could.

Mother didn't have any friends I knew of. She had worked for years in the accounting department at General Motors but quit when I was born. She didn't see her own family. Although they lived nearby, the only time I saw relatives was when her parents picked me up for the weekend, and we'd go places. A relative of ours had a horse farm and going to visit him and his family there was the best thing ever. I loved the horses, the sense of family, and being away from my house, which was as quiet, still, and lifeless as a mausoleum.

My father worked for GM, too. Everybody in Michigan worked in the auto industry at that time. He started on the line, then got a dress-up-to-go-to-work job, but he didn't like dressing up, so he asked to go back to the line. They made him the shop foreman, which he wasn't crazy about either, but it was better than an office job.

We lived in a lake house, and almost everyone who lived near us was retired. There wasn't anybody nearby who had kids. I kind of grew up like a mini-adult, because I was only around adults.

My father raised beagles when I was little, and they were my only and best friends. I loved playing with them, letting them jump all over me and lick my face. Right about the time I started school I developed allergies, and because my parents thought the dogs were the cause, the dogs had to go. I tried to suggest that maybe it was something to do with school, but my mother wasn't buying it. I was heartbroken. I felt as if it was my fault, and I was very lonely without the dogs.

My parents were not role models for a happy, healthy marriage, either. They lived separate lives. My father loved hunting, fishing, yard work, and animals. My mother stayed in the house. I'm not sure what she loved or even what she did with herself all day. How dirty could a house get with only three people—and no animals—in it? How long did it take to cook dinner for three?

My parents didn't go anywhere together socially. They both drank, but they didn't even drink together. My father drank outside the house and with his buddies, and my mother drank secretly alone at home.

I was a good student in everything but math. I read constantly. I think lots of only children did, at least before computers came along. I loved animals so much that I wanted to be a veterinarian, but my mother discouraged it because of my allergies and my struggles with math.

When I was eighteen and close to graduating from high school, my father died in a hospital in Arizona following scheduled heart surgery with a specialist. My mother had not gone with him, which kind of tells the story of their marriage and the type of person she was. He was in a hospital room by himself miles away from us when he died. I had talked to him on the phone that evening, so it was even more of a shock to me when the call came in the middle of the night. His body was flown back home for the funeral. I was devastated and had nowhere to turn for comfort, certainly not to my mother. The funeral, my graduation—it was all a blur. I can barely remember any of it.

Then it was just my mother and me, and we were like strangers. She read magazines and watched soap operas. All I wanted was to be gone.

I had earned some scholarship money and intended to go away to a state school, but my mother told me I couldn't leave—that I needed to stay home with her and enroll in the community college to be a dental hygienist. She said I would be finished in two years, and I suppose she assumed that because the most teeth anyone can have is thirty-two, I could manage the math.

I had never expressed any desire to be a dental hygienist, and I have no idea how she came up with that idea, but I was not a questioning child. I never challenged what my parents felt was the right thing for me to do. Instead, I took the passive-aggressive route: two weeks before graduating, I dropped out. I just could not overcome my revulsion at putting my hands in someone's mouth, especially in the days before everyone wore gloves. I can put my hand in a dog's mouth or a horse's mouth—and in even worse areas of an animal's body—but I could not put my fingers in a human mouth. My brilliant career as a dental hygienist was over before it began.

I didn't have a plan B, other than getting away from my mother, so I made the classic leap from frying pan to fire and married my high school sweetheart. He had joined the military after graduation; after our very small wedding, I moved to Hawaii where he was stationed. Hawaii is even more beautiful than photos make it appear, only not the part of Hawaii where we lived. We rented a dingy apartment in a rundown complex that had lots of young military couples, loud parties, and cockroaches. I had no transportation, which made it difficult to even look for work.

Along with the crummy apartment, my marriage was not exactly paradise, either. My husband was secretive, he worked strange hours, and we were always broke. As naïve as I was, it took me several months before I figured out that he was doing drugs, a lot of drugs, and I confronted him. I have always been very antidrug, and I told him he had to stop. He refused, so I used some of my savings, bought a ticket, and went home to Michigan, hoping that would make him quit. When it didn't seem to have any effect at all, I filed for divorce and was right back in the frying pan with my mother.

I got a job at the mall and another job watching kids on the playground at the elementary school I had attended. I felt like I was on a slow train to nowhere. I really didn't know what I wanted to do, other than escape my mom's house again. I wasn't making enough money at even two minimum-wage jobs, so I got married again—to the best man from my first wedding.

Paul and I had known each other since elementary school, and our relationship was comfortable and familiar. We got married at the courthouse, a civil ceremony that was very quick; and then I moved into his mobile home in a trailer park. Within a month I was pregnant. I was twenty-two, and I knew that my life had already changed— no more sleeping in, no more spontaneous trips to a restaurant or a movie, no weekend trips to the lake. I had to be responsible.

Right after Paul Junior was born, I went back to work, determined that my children would not grow up in a mobile home.

My mother volunteered to watch the baby while we worked. I got a sales job in a furniture store, then started to do some decorating for them and worked my way up to buyer. I got to go to New York to markets, and I loved it. It was exciting to be there in the city, doing something on my own. But then I got pregnant with Steven, and I decided to quit working full time so I could stay at home with my kids. Paul Senior had gotten his builder's license and was making good money. We bought a house on a small farm, and we had two ponies, some chickens, and rabbits. My habit of building menageries had begun.

We didn't intend to move specifically to Tennessee; we just knew we wanted to be somewhere warmer than Michigan. The winters were really tough there. The weather affected work for Paul, and the boys were getting older and wanted to spend more time outside. That's not much fun when it's below zero!

Paul was thinking about one of the Carolinas, but he had gone to a technical school in Nashville and also liked that area. So we put our house on the market and headed to Nashville first, with the idea of going on to see North and South Carolina. We had called a real estate agent in Middle Tennessee, because we wanted to see what small farms were like down there. He told us there were several properties that fit our criteria in a place called Lebanon. We thought he was kidding. Lebanon, Tennessee? He showed us a few places that didn't work, and we were ready to head east, but he convinced us to stay and let his wife cook supper for us. While we were eating, he went out and convinced the man down the road to sell his farm. You have to admire that kind of salesmanship. We went to see the farm and ended up buying it.

Paul was almost six and Steven was two when we settled in Tennessee. I stayed home with the kids, and Paul was working construction. We had rabbits and chickens again and then bought our first goat. I wasn't the vet I'd wanted to be when I was a young girl, but I had the animals I loved.

It was a good life, or so I thought, but Paul was working a lot, he had some issues that he didn't want to share with me, and we began to grow in very different directions. He eventually moved out, and we divorced when Steven was four and Paul not yet eight. Paul Senior was going through a kind of second childhood at that time, so I was left to raise two boys on my own on that farm. I squeaked by on child support, selling eggs and goats and eating what we raised and grew. We had a huge apple orchard, so there was a lot of apple eating—apple muffins, applesauce, stewed apples, apple pie, baked apples. I'm surprised any of us have ever eaten an apple since.

There were so many chores to do with that many animals that the boys had to help out; there was no choice. They became little men, they were so responsible for their age. We couldn't afford cable TV, but it didn't matter. The animals were our entertainment— we could watch them play for hours, and laugh at their antics. They were also our jobs, our livelihood, and an education for the boys. Paul and Steven saw babies being born and how the mother animals cared for them. They saw where food came from—not from the grocery store or a fast-food restaurant but out of the earth. They understood that a hamburger came from a cow, that hot dogs came from a pig, that fried chicken came from a chicken that had started as an egg and that may have been walking around the yard two days earlier. There was no luxury in our lives. It was hard work, but I remember those days as such happy times. It made us very close.

It's funny to Bernie and me how similar the arcs of our lives were prior to meeting each other. He was also an only child, although he had more relatives around, and I don't think he was as lonely and isolated as I was. We were both solidly middle class; our parents were hardworking and fairly strict. Spanking was an approved form of punishment back then, and Dr. Spock was still regarded by many as a little bit out there—especially to Bernie's parents, who had been born and raised in Germany. Bernie was born there, too, but he and his family moved to America before he turned three. They ended up in North Hollywood, California, which wasn't anything like the Hollywood everyone knows from the movies.

His father worked as a carpenter; he had his own business. His mom was a claims adjuster for an insurance agency until his father's business grew and she came on to run the front office. His father didn't want German spoken in the house because he wanted to be sure that Bernie spoke English. He also made sure that Bernie learned carpentry, just by watching him and working with him. In the summers, Bernie's dad farmed him out to subcontractors, so he learned plumbing and electrical work, too. He wanted to go to college, but his father had very bad arthritis and relied on Bernie a lot. It wasn't in their culture to rebel against their parents, so, like me, he did what his parents wanted him to do and kind of segued from working after school and on weekends to working full time.

He got married the first time when he was twenty and his wife was only sixteen. She also saw marriage as a way out of her house. As soon as she graduated from high school, she got pregnant and had their first son, Shawn, and then Ryan a little more than a year after that. She was still a child herself, and when Ryan was only eight months old, she walked out on all of them.

So there was Bernie, a twenty-two-year-old single father. It was really hard for him. During the three years before his mom finally stopped working to watch the boys for him, he went through nineteen babysitters. I give him so much credit, to take on that kind of responsibility at his age. It really shows his character. His ex-wife rarely saw her boys, and she certainly didn't pay child support, although she did harangue him simply out of meanness, often calling social services to report him as neglectful or negligent. The inspector would come to the trailer and find it clean and neat, dinner on the stove, and Bernie folding clothes while his boys took a bath. Bernie was father and mother to them, as much as he could be.

He admits that some of the relationships he had then were more about getting a mom for his kids than a partner for himself, which had a predictable result. His second marriage was to a woman a few years older than him whom he'd met in church. She wanted kids of her own, and they really tried, but it never happened, and I'm sure that was hard on her.

They ended up in Nashville after she saw a segment on *Oprah* called "50 Fabulous Places to Raise Your Family." Nashville and Phoenix were the two places that appealed to her, and Bernie didn't want to go to Phoenix, so he and his wife came to Nashville, right around the same time that Paul Senior and I did. We laugh that we have Oprah Winfrey to thank for our being together.

Bernie's second wife didn't think Nashville was so fabulous, though. After they spent about four years together, she ended up leaving, so it was just Bernie and the boys again.

I had gone to work for my ex-husband Paul, who had a construction company that specialized in trim. I did doorknobs. I have no idea what skills I possessed that translated to doorknobs, but it was good work. Every building needs a door, and every door needs a doorknob. I would get up at Dark-Thirty o'clock every morning, do the farm chores, get the kids up, get them ready for school and onto the bus, race to work, do a half-day, dash home to be there when they got off the bus, supervise homework, make dinner, do chores, and fall into bed. Then I'd get up and do it all again the next day.

Bernie and I met on the job; there was nothing at all romantic about it. We were both seeing other people at the time, and he was a smoker, which is a deal breaker for me. Yet that gave us a chance to become friends first, and we became really good friends. This was a first for both of us in a relationship. He would talk about his girlfriend troubles and challenges as a single parent, and I would do the same. We saw each other all day on the job and then talked on the phone for a couple of hours after our kids went to bed.

As time went on, I think we both began to see the possibility of a relationship, although I was probably more hesitant than he was. There were his kids, for one thing. Maybe it was because they were being raised by a single dad, but I had a problem with some of their behaviors. Bernie's boys were older than mine, so I was afraid they might influence my boys to be age-inappropriate.

But eventually Bernie won me over. He quit smoking to seal the deal, and we were married on March 31, 1997, at the Baptist church Bernie attended in Franklin. It was very simple: the four boys and just a few friends. The church was feeding the homeless that night, so we ate our wedding dinner with them. That felt right to us. We didn't have the money for a honeymoon, so we just went home after our dinner with the homeless. At least, we had a home.

I think I got pregnant that very night. We definitely didn't plan it—we had quite enough on our plates, and we didn't feel a driving need to have a child together. Bernie was under the impression from the fertility doctor he and his second wife had seen that his siring days were over. At least, that's what he told me. Surprise! But we embraced the news as God's plan and celebrated William's arrival the week before Christmas.

Blending the families was a bit of a challenge, and we probably should have done a little more prep work on that. The boys had gotten along fine before we were married, but when my sons and I moved into Bernie's tiny three-bedroom house, things got tense. Steven and Paul were used to sharing, but Shawn and Ryan had previously had their own rooms. Shawn was sixteen years old and had always taken on a lot of responsibility for running their house. In hindsight it's understandable that he might get upset at a relatively strange woman coming into his house and taking his job, on top of being forced to share his father and his bedroom. There was definitely some tension. When we moved to a larger house, Shawn had the whole basement to himself, and we just tried to stay out of each other's way. Thankfully, the misunderstandings between us lessened when Shawn went to live with his mother, who had settled in Atlanta.

Then we moved again, to a huge old house that had been converted into rental units. It had six apartments, six bathrooms, and six kitchens. Restricted to the no-budget plan, we did everything ourselves to turn it back into a single family home. It took us almost four years of backbreaking work on nights and weekends before we finished that house. It consumed every waking moment, and it was a showcase when it was done.

But we wanted warmer weather. Paul kept getting bronchitis every winter, so we thought a change in climate might help. We had driven through Florida a year earlier on vacation, down one coast and up another. We liked the west coast of the state better—the Gulf water was warmer, shallower, and calmer than the ocean, which we thought was better for Willie. He was only three, and the Atlantic was very rough. We found the kind of small-town community we liked in Fort Myers Beach, so in October 2002 we put our Tennessee home on the market, packed everything up, and moved to Florida, the Sunshine State.

2

Seeking

The easygoing lifestyle in Fort Myers Beach suited us well. We walked, biked, swam in our pool or a neighbor's pool, went to the beach, and played in the park. We had a small, partly pebbled yard, so there wasn't much upkeep involved, and the house—compared to other rehab projects we had taken on—was finished. We grilled outdoors a lot and loved to eat on our second-floor deck that overlooked a canal where we could watch the manatees play. Anytime we could be outside, that's where you would find us.

Willie was in a good school, Steven was close to graduating and had a part-time job that he loved because it was on the beach, Bernie had steady work, and I was a happy housewife. Yet my desire for another child kept tugging at me.

Some little things came up that moved the process along for Bernie. We were attending a Baptist church on the beach in Florida and got a new pastor. He and his wife had four kids of their own and wanted to adopt a baby from China. The wife and I talked about it frequently. She already knew that I was interested in adoption but that Bernie was reluctant. Maybe she thought it was something that would be easier to do with another couple. I talked to Bernie about it, and he said that if we adopted, there were probably plenty of kids in Florida who needed a home. That "if" gave me hope, and I sensed that he was softening.

Our church had a retreat center on the beach, and if it wasn't being used by the church or rented out to another group, the pastor invited the Florida Baptist Children's Home to bring out some of its children for the weekend. It was such a fun thing for them and a break in their routine; they got to swim in the ocean, play on the beach. The retreat has a kitchen and a dorm and is very simple.

When the kids from the home were there for a weekend, families from the church would send out food for them, so that when the kids got there, everything was taken care of. Usually, we'd just drive the food over and drop it off, but Steven volunteered to go and teach the kids to skim board. He is really good at it, and lots of those kids had never been to the ocean, much less on a skim board. Steven ended up staying all day and had a blast, but I noticed that he was really quiet on the drive home.

That night at dinner, Steven talked about how sad it was, all of those great kids without families, and how he wished he could take them home with him. I think Bernie was really touched by these kind words coming out of the mouth of a teenager! I could see tears in his eyes and sensed another stone being laid on his path.

I didn't want to push it, but I couldn't resist a nudge every now and then. With all of the four older boys except Steven moved out and his exit right around the corner, I pointed out to Bernie how quiet it was getting around the house. That didn't seem to bother him a bit, although when I added that Steven's departure would leave Willie an only child for at least the next decade, it hit a nerve, as Bernie remembered the loneliness of having no siblings.

Not long afterward, we were visiting with the preacher and his wife after church, and she filled us in on their adoption quest. As we walked away, Bernie turned and looked at me and asked, "Do you still want to adopt a child?" I couldn't believe it. I searched his face to see if he was serious. He took me by the shoulders, looked me in the eyes, and said he was ready.

So, I was ready, he was ready, and Willie loved the idea of having a brother or a sister closer to his age whom he could play with.

We may have been ready, but we had a lot to learn. Knowing how many children are in the world waiting for adoption, lots of people think that once you decide to adopt, you call an agency and children start arriving on your doorstep. In Miami-Dade County alone, there were about four hundred boys and four hundred girls ready and available to be adopted. In one county! That didn't count the kids in foster care who, for various reasons, were not available for adoption.

We did it all backward. First, we searched for a child, then we found out that we couldn't even be considered for adoption until we had our Home Study done by an agency and completed our MAPP (Model Approach to Partnership & Parenting) classes.

We wanted to move quickly—and I didn't want to give Bernie too much time or a reason to change his mind—so we went through a private agency to have our Home Study done. If we had gone through the county, it could have taken two or three years; instead, we paid $1,200 to have it done privately, and it took about three months.

While we were waiting for the Home Study to be done, we started our MAPP classes, ten weeks of weekly classes. People get discouraged because they don't want to wait three years, they don't have $1,200, or they have a hard time fitting in the MAPP classes. It is hard, and it is a lot to do, but it's worth so much in the long run. Bernie and I learned a lot in the MAPP classes. Before we went, we thought that after five kids, we knew it all.

The Home Study is extensive, as it should be. The state is entrusting you with a life and can't just take your word for it that you're adopting out of the goodness of your heart or that you are stable, have an adequate home, and are financially prepared to raise a child. It's too bad there are no requirements like that before people get pregnant.

We were fingerprinted and had criminal background checks. Happily, all of us had clean records, and the state didn't unearth any rattling skeletons in our closet worse than making mistakes in our previous spouses. We had to get reference letters from neighbors, relatives, and our pastor. We had to produce copies of our divorce papers, which was a problem for Bernie because he had burned his, so he had to contact records offices in California to get proof that he was not a bigamist.

The adoption officials made home visits, called our employers, checked our financial records, and interviewed all of the kids many times, as well as their teachers and employers and the people who wrote letters on our behalf. The older boys were getting irritated, but Willie just got more excited as it began to seem real to him. Steven was closest to him in age, but he was still ten years older. Willie thought he would have a playmate, someone to go on bike rides through the neighborhood and go to the beach and play board games with.

When the Home Study and the MAPP classes are finished, and you are ready to start considering children, there is a checklist to go over. Would you take an African American child, a blind child, a mixed-race child, a disabled child, an older child? All of these are called special needs children and are harder to place. We knew we wanted an older child, and we thought the color of his or her skin would be such a small thing, compared to what so many of these children have been through.

The adoption officials had told us to be very aware of birth order. We didn't want to bring a child into the home who was older than Willie. We definitely didn't want a baby. We wanted a child we wouldn't have to potty train and who would sleep through the night. We didn't want a child who had been sexually abused or who was severely mentally challenged. So much of what we were looking for—in fact, most of what we were looking for—was based on how Willie would interact with that child and how it would affect him.

I became obsessed with looking at available children online. It seems like an odd way to do it, searching online for a child as if you were looking for a car or a boat or a dog. But it's become the norm, and it's actually very informative and practical. A lot of kids sounded promising, but then we'd make further inquiries and find out they couldn't be around other children or around animals. One little girl we asked about—who looked like an angel—had gone through several disrupted adoptions and was sent back to the agency because she consistently attacked the mother in every home. She had issues with other females. We found siblings—seven and eight years old—who seemed great online, but we found out they had been sent to homes and had come back five times. There was another girl who urinated all over the furniture whenever she got upset. There were other kids who mistreated or tortured animals.

Some of the kids had already spent time in mental hospitals. Others had been through so much that they would never be able to function as normal members of society. It is heartbreaking, but you have to protect the family you have.

We were getting discouraged. We became more open on some conditions and more opposed to others. Some of the answers on our checklist changed from no to maybe and some from maybe to no. Some yeses became maybes.

Then we got a call from the woman who had worked with us on our Home Study. She told us about a Heart Gallery event coming up in Tampa and suggested that we see some kids live and in person. We decided to give it a try.

3

The Girl in the Photo

It is 160 miles from our quiet little subdivision in Fort Myers Beach to Ybor City, but on a late fall morning in 2006, it seemed like it was taking Bernie and me forever to get from point A to point B. As it turned out, that three-hour drive was the easiest part of the journey we were starting.

Willie was in the backseat and already bored, but Bernie and I were anxious. Navigating through the narrow streets of this unfamiliar area was challenging enough, but knowing that once we parked the car and walked into GameWorks, we would be stepping into completely uncharted territory was unnerving.

We knew about the Heart Gallery of Tampa Bay from our online searches for adoptable children. Children who are available for adoption and are selected to participate have a portrait taken by a professional photographer, which is then put online in the Heart Gallery with a couple of paragraphs of information and usually a bit of audio from the child. "My name is Ian, I'm twelve years old,

I get good grades in school, my favorite subject is science, I play baseball and hope to grow up to be a major leaguer."

The event in Ybor City was going to be a live version of the website. There would be kids in foster care who were available for adoption onsite for prospective adoptive parents to meet in person and spend some time with. People could get more information about children they were interested in. It was supposed to be "fun," but we were not having fun yet.

We are not arcade kind of people. My boys had no time for video games when they were smaller and the three of us were living in the country. There were too many chores to be done after school and in between homework, dinner, and bedtime. When Bernie and I married and we still lived in Tennessee, it seemed like we always had some big project going on, and the boys were expected to pitch in.

In my opinion, an arcade is like a kiddie-size version of casinos. Artificially lit, cacophonous, frenetic, addictive, and a big waste of money. We left daylight behind and walked into a cavernous room filled with loud machines, blinking neon lights, simulated weapons, junk food, and about a hundred kids from toddlers to teens showing clear proof of the effects of all of those. This is your brain on arcade.

But for the Heart Gallery, there is a method to the madness. The crazy environment provides a distraction from the reality of this event—these are children who for the most part have been abused, neglected, abandoned, or literally thrown away. They are on display, jostling one another for a position, looking for ways to stand out, auditioning to become a part of what is known in the adoption world as a "forever family." I thought it was like a bad combination of speed dating and *Survivor*.

Everybody loves babies. What's not to love? There they lie, swaddled in soft, pastel-colored blankets, with round cheeks, adorable toothless gums and hairless fuzzy heads, little fingers reaching for yours, perfect little toes, cooing and babbling. Like precious little puppies and kittens, minus fur, fangs, and claws.

But even the four-year-olds here looked big to us. Bernie and I are both pretty compact—he is barely 5'6" and I can still wear girls' jeans. Not surprisingly, given the gene pool, Willie is small for his age and probably always will be. I could tell that some of the kids were also eight or even younger, and they towered over him and outweighed him by at least ten pounds, if not more. We couldn't bring a giant into Willie's wee world.

And they were so loud! Though Willie can bend my ear for hours about a beetle he saw on the deck or what might happen if he was hit on the head by a falling mango from our neighbor's tree, he was by nature a quiet child, not prone to yelling or shrieking.

But we had just driven three hours, we were there, and we were determined to see it through. Families and children were divided into groups. During the event, the groups rotated, so that everyone had a chance to interact for a brief time with everyone else. You also got to see the kids interacting with one another and playing in a casual environment. The children all wore name tags, and the adults were each given a card. If you were interested in a particular child or group of siblings, you put their names on the card and went to a table staffed by agency employees, and they would give you more information on those children.

The younger kids were playing and having fun. They were just excited to get unlimited access to games, eat pizza, and run around like lunatics. But the older kids knew the score. They walked right up to you, introduced themselves, told you where they went to school, what grade they were in, how they were doing, and what their interests were. They wanted loving parents and a healthy, safe home so desperately, it seemed like they might burst with their yearning.

They all needed families, they all deserved families, and in a perfect world, they would all walk out of GameWorks hand in hand with their forever families to live happily ever after.

At the same time, it was just overwhelming. After two hours, Bernie was getting cranky—no doubt, he was thinking about how nice a peaceful one-child house would be. Willie looked uncomfortable, and my head was pounding. We had written two names on our card—a seventeen-year-old boy who we later found out was adopted by an older couple, and a fourteen-year-old girl whom we ended up crossing off our list when she was joined by her extremely hyperactive younger brother. The girl was darling and her brother was sweet, but Willie had just been diagnosed with attention-deficit/hyperactivity disorder (ADHD), and we felt that adding such a hyperactive boy to our family would not be good for him. We were all getting a little discouraged.

I was ready to call it a day, but before we left, I went to the Heart Gallery desk to see if there was any information or a brochure we could take home with us. That's when I saw the picture of the little girl on the board behind the table. Her photo didn't look like any of the other Heart Gallery portraits, which were all in color and taken outdoors under trees, beside a flower bed, or near a pond. Some of these children held dolls, others clutched footballs, and a few carried books. All had big smiles on their faces and were dressed in their Sunday best.

The photo of the little girl was grainy black and white, even a little blurred. There was no pretty background behind her, no fun prop, and no cute outfit. In fact, I couldn't tell what she was wearing, if anything. The dark hair framing her pale face didn't even look combed or particularly clean, her bangs were uneven and jaggedly cut, and she wasn't smiling. She had a vacant, distant look in her eyes. Even so, she was pretty in a very frail way and had a beautiful mouth. But it was those eyes that pulled me in and grabbed my heart. I knew I hadn't seen her among the children that day and I wondered why. Maybe she was sick?

I looked around for Bernie and found him standing over Willie at a game, practically asleep on his feet, despite all of the noise.

I grabbed his arm and told him I thought I had found a child. He perked up and looked around the room. "Where? A boy or a girl?" I told him it was a little girl. He asked again where she was. I told him that she wasn't exactly there, as in present in the room. She was in a photograph. He looked at me like I was crazy.

"There are a hundred live kids right here. Why do you want the one in a photo?" I took him over to the board and pointed at the little girl in the picture. I could tell he was moved and possibly even a little bit curious but skeptical. Who could blame him?

I got in line, and he went to grab Willie, who didn't have a clue what was going on. When we all made it to the desk, I pointed at the photo and asked who she was and why she wasn't there. The woman glanced back over her shoulder and said, "Danielle? Oh, she couldn't handle something like this. She is not used to being around this many people." Then she looked around us and gestured to the next couple who had a filled-out card. We were dismissed.

I took Bernie's hand, and we went to the back of the line. When we got to the front again, I asked more questions. The people were nice but were getting a little frustrated with me. We were told that the girl came from a horrible situation, that the damage she had suffered before being taken into state custody was likely permanent. The more the staff tried to steer us toward other children, the more determined I was to know more about the little girl named Danielle.

Finally, one woman looked me in the eye and said, "Trust me. Raising this child will be a lifelong struggle. You just don't want her."

I felt hopeful for the first time that day. If you tell Bernie and me that we can't do something, we will do everything in our power to prove you wrong. After we heard those words, I knew Bernie would jump on board. How was this little girl ever going to find her way to a real home if everyone was told the same thing? I looked at my husband and said, "Bernie, she needs us." He answered, "I know."

We both knew. It wasn't a clap of thunder or a bolt of lightning kind of revelation. There was no sense of "Eureka! We've found her!"

It was a calm and serene moment, an answer to our prayer, although not quite the one we thought we were praying for.

4

The Feral Child

All the way home from the Heart Gallery event, Bernie and I talked about Danielle. On Monday, I began making calls to the agency. We weren't told much, just that after she was removed from her mother's home a year earlier, she was in the hospital for about three weeks and then was placed in a therapeutic foster home. The mother had appealed the termination of parental rights, but no one believed she would win, so the agency continued with the adoption process and added her to the Heart Gallery.

The agency officials said they would look over our Home Study and make sure that we would be eligible to adopt Danielle if the time came. We were happy to have made even that little bit of progress, but their examination of our qualifications was taking forever. Bernie started to pester them, calling the agency to ask what was happening and why it was taking so long.

While we were on vacation in St. Augustine, we got a call from a woman named Garet White, who was the adoption case manager assigned to Danielle. She had been at GameWorks that day, but neither Bernie nor I could place her. I'm sure everyone remembered us, the annoying crazy people who wanted to meet Danielle. Garet told us that she would be the liaison between us and Danielle and the agency and that the next step—should we decide to take it—was an in-person meeting with Danielle. She told us that would take place at Sanders Memorial Elementary in Land O' Lakes, where Danielle was enrolled. All that we wanted to know was how soon this would happen.

Garet asked us to do one thing for her first: rent the movie *Nell*, watch it, and then call her back to let her know if we were still interested in Danielle. I had heard of the movie, but none of us had seen it. I called Paul and asked him to go to the video store and pick it up, then to come over and watch it with us. I popped a big bowl of popcorn, and we all sat down in front of the television as if we were about to watch *The Sound of Music*.

The opening scenes of the mountains of North Carolina were breathtaking. We've never been to the mountains, and Bernie remarked that we should take a vacation there someday. At the beginning of the movie, a boy in a bicycle bumps down dirt paths to a cabin, where he is bringing a box of groceries. I was thinking, "What a beautiful place to live, so peaceful!" The mood in our living room changed pretty abruptly when the camera found the dead elderly woman on the floor, two fresh daisies covering her eyes. It spooked the boys and startled us. Now we didn't know what to expect.

Neither do the doctor and the sheriff, who come to the house to remove the body. The sheriff is vaguely familiar with the woman, who has lived for years as a hermit in a backwoods cabin with no electricity or running water. But while they're in the cabin, they find that the old woman has not lived alone when a young woman bursts in on them like a wild animal before running off into the woods. She turns out to be the woman's daughter, one of twin girls;

her sister died when she was young. The later scene where Nell shows the doctor her sister's skeleton in a cave—with daisies over her eyes—was so sad, we were all crying.

The doctor goes back again and again, trying to win Nell's trust. She has never been exposed to the outside world, she flails out at anyone who comes near her, she can scream like a beast, and when she does speak, it's a strange language she acquired through listening to her mother's garbled speech, caused by a stroke. Whew!

After the movie was over, we all sat there, quiet and drained. Only half of the popcorn had been eaten. Paul turned to Bernie and me and said out loud what Steven and Willie were probably thinking, "Are you two insane? Have you lost your minds?"

I got up and went to the computer. In the movie, when the doctor brought a psychiatrist to meet Nell and she reported on the woman to her colleagues, they described her as a feral child. They seemed quite delighted at the discovery, calling it rare and practically unheard of. I had heard the term but wasn't exactly sure what it meant. I thought that even the word—*feral*—sounded ugly.

I Googled "feral child." There were more than fifty thousand entries, and not one looked good. Wild, undomesticated, isolated from human contact, with little or no experience of human care, loving or social behavior, or human language. Some children had actually been abandoned and then raised by animals, and others were confined by their parents and denied interactions with others. There were famous stories of feral children from hundreds of years ago, like the boy raised with wolves, and fictional stories like *Tarzan: King of the Jungle*. Even more disturbing were the stories of children who are still alive now, like Genie, who was tied to a potty chair for ten years, and Oxana, who from the time she was three years old lived in a kennel behind her family's home, raised with dogs.

My head was spinning. What was Garet trying to tell us? By the time I turned off the computer, Paul had left and everyone else had gone to bed. I looked in on Steven, pulled the sheet up around Willie, and kissed the top of his head. I got into bed beside Bernie and nudged him awake. "Bernie!" I whispered. "What are we going to do?" He opened one eye and looked at me. "Tomorrow, we're going to call Garet and tell her we want to meet Danielle. Right now, I'm going back to sleep." And he rolled over and did just that. I lay in bed awake for a long time, trying to remember Danielle's pale face in the photo, wondering whether we were doing the right thing in even starting this, and praying for help and guidance. It was nearly dawn when I finally dozed off. Before Bernie left for work, he called Garet and asked her to set a date for our first meeting.

5

Meeting Danielle

Within a week, Garet called and told us she had made arrangements for us to meet Danielle in her classroom. Willie wanted to come along, but Bernie and I decided it would be best for just the two of us to meet Danielle for the first time. We didn't want to overwhelm her, for one thing. For another, even though we didn't say it out loud, in the back of our minds both of us were thinking that anything could go wrong.

Would the feeling that we'd both had about her when we saw her photo at GameWorks still be there when we saw her in person? What if we saw her and decided—even if only one of us decided—that she was just too much? What if her history, which we still didn't know, made it impossible for her to blend in with our family? What if she might cause harm to Willie? We had heard some real horror stories during the months we were looking at children. Considering what some of those children had been through, you couldn't blame them for acting out and becoming violent or sexual predators. But we simply couldn't have anyone like that in our home.

We had no idea what to expect. Was she going to be like Nell? Speaking a strange language, flying around like a bird, running off, dancing by herself to music that only she heard in her head? We were very anxious, but we were also excited. The waiting was finally about to be over, and we were going to meet Danielle. I kept having to tell Bernie to slow down, we wanted to get there in one piece!

Our first stop was to meet Garet White at her office in the agency where she worked. Bernie had spoken to her several times on the phone, but I never had. She wasn't at all what I expected, which was something along the lines of a big, imposing, tough-as-nails spinster. Definitely not someone so pretty, serene, and soft-spoken. There was something very tender and nurturing about her, and I guessed that she was probably a mother herself. In fact, she was a single mom of a young son, whose pictures decorated her office.

We were running late, so, rather than go through the documentation and the disclosure then, we went right to Sanders Memorial Elementary School in Land O' Lakes where Danielle was enrolled. It was the one school closest to her foster home that offered exceptional student education (ESE) and bus service. The school looked like it had been expanded and added on to in kind of a willy-nilly fashion. The office was in a squat building that had been the original school, cinder blocks painted white, with windows trimmed in royal blue. Other buildings were in various architectural styles and eras, but all of the campus was shaded by towering old trees draped with Spanish moss. It was very welcoming, and we felt good that Danielle was in a place like this and not in something cold and institutional.

Garet had been to the school many times to check on Danielle, so she was well known there. She introduced us to the school principal, Jill Middleton, and we made small talk while we waited for Marisa Perez, the behavior specialist for the school. We had glimpsed Ms. Perez's back as she ran out the rear door to answer a summons on her walkie-talkie to track down two fourth-graders who were MIA from the classroom. I had a feeling that those kids didn't have a chance.

Principal Middleton told us that Ms. Perez had bonded very strongly with Danielle and, when she had a meltdown, was able to calm her by taking the child onto her lap in the rocking chair. My mind flashed back to when I rocked my boys for the same reason—but they were infants and toddlers at the time. Danielle had just turned eight.

Ms. Perez whooshed back into the office, hugging Bernie and me as if we were old friends she couldn't be happier to see. She was the type of person who could probably bond with a bear; she practically surged with positive energy. Although we hadn't yet met Danielle, so far we were impressed with the people who were caring for her.

Principal Middleton walked along with us to Danielle's classroom, and as we passed other members of the staff, they greeted us with big smiles. I didn't realize until later that everyone knew we were coming to meet Danielle and probably thought we were either insane or saints. Bernie would say that we definitely leaned more toward the former than the latter.

Along the way, Principal Middleton told us that Danielle was in Kevin O'Keefe's classroom for children with profound needs and that Danielle was considered profoundly mentally handicapped, or PMR. As we had discovered when we started thinking of adoption, you could fill an entire dictionary with acronyms used by the foster care and child services system. Now we would be learning new ones related to special education. Mr. O'Keefe had been in the field for nearly twenty years, more than ten at Sanders, and was beloved by his students and even more by their parents.

As we walked, I was only half listening, trying to calm the butterflies in my stomach. I hadn't been so nervous about meeting someone since the one time I agreed to go on a blind date. What if the very sight of us set off a "fit," and Ms. Perez had to spring into action?

I don't think we were prepared for what we saw when Principal Middleton opened the door and we walked into the classroom. Unless you have an extremely disabled or very mentally challenged member of your family or you work in that field in some way, you can't possibly be prepared. Most of us have been taught since we were small children not to stare at other people, whether it is someone with a terrible birthmark or scar, someone missing a limb, or a person who is handicapped or is obviously emotionally unstable. It becomes an automatic response—look away, avert your eyes, don't stare!

But when you enter a classroom that is exclusively for children with profound needs, there is nowhere to look except at what is right before your eyes. I had to make a conscious effort not to look away, to walk mindfully into this world that was so extraordinarily different from what I knew with my three boys and what most parents' elementary school experience has been.

In this classroom, there was no teacher writing vocabulary words on the blackboard for students to copy. There were no seven-year-olds jumping up to wave their hands in the air, hoping to be called on to answer a math question. No one was bent over a book or drawing a picture or whispering and giggling with a friend.

Instead, there were children in wheelchairs and children belted into chairs pulled up to tables. One boy was strapped to a board that was upright but tilted at an angle. There were two children on mats, one lying on his back with his arms out to his side as if he was making a snow angel, and another on his side, with a rolled pillow bracing him. None of them spoke a word, and it was impossible to tell whether they were even aware of our presence.

It was a large room, with several defined areas and adaptive furnishings and equipment. It was brightly painted in multiple primary colors, and nothing had sharp edges. Aides were showing pictures to children or reading to them. One aide stood beside a small sink with a little girl, running water over her hands as the girl's head lolled to one side.

We looked for Danielle. After the event in Tampa, Heart Gallery had put a new photo of her on its website. She was wearing a white T-shirt and her hair was neatly combed, cut to just above her jaw line with bangs trimmed to almost touch her brows. Garet had picked her up from school one day, taken her to the photographer's studio, and made crazy faces until they got a bit of a smile from her.

Even without the updated photo for reference, it would have been obvious which of the children was Danielle. She was one of the few who were mobile, and she was exceedingly mobile. In fact, she never stopped moving. Lithe and long-limbed, she walk-bounced on her tip-toes, her arms rigid but swinging back and forth at her sides. She would go over to one activity center, play with something, put it down, go to the blocks, put one in her mouth, put it down, go to another, pick up a ball, put it down, go over to a table, take a drink from a sippy cup, and drop it, which explained why it was tied to a leg of the table.

It didn't seem like she even noticed us, although she looked at Garet and Ms. Perez when they called her name and let Garet give her a little hug. We said, "Hello, Danielle," but she turned away and skittered off. She reminded me of Tigger from the Winnie the Pooh books, bouncing all over the place.

The sun around which this alternate universe revolved was Kevin O'Keefe. Tall and slim, soft-spoken and bearded, with kind eyes and a reserved manner, he offered a shy smile when we were introduced. He seemed a bit wary of us, but in hindsight, I know he was being protective of Danielle. He genuinely cared about all of his students and, as we found out later, keeps in touch with their families long after they leave his classroom.

Garet asked whether he and Ms. Perez could sit with Bernie and me and tell us about Danielle—what she did in the classroom, what she was learning to do, and what their goals for her were. Mr. O'Keefe told us about her need to move—something that was quite obvious already—and said that as long as she didn't feel penned in or restrained, she was generally happy. He said that she came to the classroom drinking from a bottle and had progressed to the sippy cup. He laughed as he told us how many times they had chased that cup until an aide came up with the idea of tying the handle to the table leg. He said that she was making progress in learning not to take other people's food. Note to self: Keep her away from Willie's plate. He's so small, he needs all the food he can get.

Mr. O'Keefe told us,

When Danielle came into my classroom last year, it was the first time she had ever been in a school setting or any kind of classroom with other children. We were told she had never been to day care or Sunday School or any kind of program for children. The school year had already started, but she had to get her immunizations before she could enroll, since she never had any. In her evaluation for qualification for Exceptional Student Evaluation, her primary exceptionality was noted to be profoundly mentally handicapped, so that's how she came to be with me, and I was glad to have her.

At first, she was almost constantly very agitated, always moving. She was in constant motion. We tried to get her outside as much as possible, so she had lots of opportunity for movement.

She did have some severe emotional outbursts. The first time we saw one, we thought there was something terribly wrong with her or that something had happened, so we called the foster mother, and she just said, No, that's how she handles her emotions.

She really wanted to eat, that was one of the first things I noticed about her. Anything she could put her hands on.

We had to be very watchful because whatever was around her, she would put in her mouth. She would take other children's food, whatever was within her reach. It took a long time to get her to stop that. She ate with her hands and would just grab food and push it all into her mouth.

The first time I took her out, she didn't know how to climb the steps to get up to the playground. We really had to assist her. We went over to the slide and helped her get up the first time, and she had no fear of going down the slide. She loved it and did it again. She picked it up very quickly, and that was surprising to me. I thought that showed a higher level of intelligence than we previously thought, in that she did pick it up so quickly.

She also developed good balancing skills. As you can see, there are children in my room lying on mats, and she was able to walk around them without losing her balance or disturbing them, which many of my children can't do. She likes to climb and get on top of things.

She has never been an aggressive child, she never hit or bit another child. There were other kids in my class who did those kinds of things. But never Danielle. Even if she was hit by another child, she did not hit back. There has always been a true sweetness about her.

While Mr. O'Keefe was talking and the aides were busy with the other children, Bernie saw his opening. Or his chance to escape. He is not big on group discussions, and although I knew he was interested in what Mr. O'Keefe had to say, Bernie's not a talker, he's a doer. He started to follow Danielle around the rooms as she made her rounds. He kept his distance. I know he didn't want to frighten her, but she didn't really seem to notice him. She picked up a Slinky and got into the swing that was suspended from the ceiling in the middle of the room. Bernie got down on one knee in front of her and smiled. "Do you want to play?" he asked and pulled on the Slinky in her hand, which pulled her forward. When he let it go, the swing went back. He pulled the Slinky, and she swung forward. He let go, and she swung back.

All of the adults in the room had stopped talking to watch them, and we saw the moment that Danielle connected with Bernie for the first time. As he smiled at her, she looked directly into his eyes and pulled the Slinky from him. He pulled, she pulled back. She was playing with Bernie.

Mr. O'Keefe and Ms. Perez smiled at each other, the aides smiled at Bernie, and Garet and I both had tears in our eyes. Such a simple little thing, but a small miracle had just taken place in that classroom. Danielle had never taken so quickly and naturally to anyone, they told us, and that revelation was all it took to put hope in our hearts.

When it was time for lunch, one of the aides asked whether we would mind feeding Danielle. Bernie and I were surprised that she wasn't self-feeding yet. We cut her sandwich into bite-size pieces because otherwise she put the entire sandwich in her mouth. Likewise with the orange sections and the carrots. We had to make sure she didn't cram another one in before she swallowed the first. Sometimes she took something and put it in her mouth herself, and other times we held a sandwich piece in front of her face and she opened her mouth like a little bird. But she wasn't eating baby food like many of the other children, and she had no lack of appetite.

After lunch, the children needed to be changed, and when the aide came over to fetch her, I offered to do it. All of my boys had toilet trained early, so I had not changed a diaper in about five years, and that was on a toddler. I picked up Danielle, laid her down on a large changing table, and pulled up the skirt she was wearing. She was oblivious, and that seemed so strange to me. She should have been embarrassed that she was wearing a diaper and that a total stranger was preparing to change her. I reached automatically for a baby wipe, and the reality of the situation hit me. Here was an eight-year-old girl having her diaper changed, and that seemed so horrible to me. Tears came into my eyes again.

It was as if she could sense what I was feeling and my anxiety, because as soon as I took her diaper off, she started screaming at the top of her lungs, as if I was murdering her. It was terrifying. I froze for a second, and then I thought, "Well, someone's been doing this for her one way or another for her entire life. She's gotten used to it, and it's no big deal to her. So just get over it and do it."

I said, "I'm sorry to upset you, Danielle, but we have to change that diaper." She stopped screaming. I used the baby wipe, put on a dry diaper, and pulled her skirt back down, and she swung her legs over the table and onto the floor. Off she went on her toes to find her Slinky. I took a deep breath, and as I turned around, I saw Bernie, smiling at me from across the room. He looked absolutely delighted, and I didn't know whether I wanted to hit him or hug him. But he had a look on his face that said, "Don't worry so much, Diane. We'll be fine. We can do this." It was a look I had seen many times in our marriage, and he had always been right.

6

Falling through the Cracks

When we left the classroom, we told Danielle we would see her again soon, but it didn't seem to make an impression on her one way or the other. We said good-bye to Mr. O'Keefe and Ms. Perez and also told them we'd be back soon. I'm not sure if they believed us.

We were tired and hungry and had a long drive ahead. Our friend Evie Barnes had kept Willie after school for us and would make sure he did his homework, but I knew he would be dying to hear about Danielle and the visit and wouldn't go to bed until we got home.

We probably would have gone to a drive-through and hit the road, except that we still had official agency business to attend to. The next step in the procedure was for Garet to do "Disclosure," which meant giving us all of the information the agency had in Danielle's file. It sounded very official and a little bit scary.

Part of us wanted to know all of it, and another part wished that we could just burn the file and start fresh. We had heard some things about bug bites and the condition of the house, but that was all we knew. We thought it had to be pretty bad for her to be removed from the home.

We drove to a Chili's restaurant, sat down at a table, ordered, and talked a bit about the visit. Garet thought it had gone well, and so did we. Still, it seemed like our chatter was just delaying the inevitable, and Bernie—in that direct way he has—finally said, "Well, let's get to it."

Garet reached into a folder and pulled out a stapled sheaf of papers. She gave us a copy and kept a copy for herself. The title page said *Study of the Child Danielle Ann Crockett*. I gasped when I saw the photo on the front—it was the same one I had seen at GameWorks. I was amazed at how different Danielle looked in the classroom a year or so later. It made me sad to see that picture again; she looked so vulnerable and lost.

Garet put a small tape recorder on the table—required procedure—then turned it on and began reading aloud. This way, the potential parents couldn't say that they were misled or not told something. I read along with our copy while Bernie listened to Garet.

The report began with the biological family, headed by the mother, a forty-nine-year-old white woman who had two sons while living in Las Vegas with her husband before being widowed in 1997. Not long after he died, Danielle was conceived through a "very brief affair," so brief that the mother didn't know the man's name.

I read the sentence again. Even before Danielle was born, there was a huge missing piece in her history, one that would never be found. She would never know her birth father's name, what color his eyes were, whether he was short or tall, or how he made a living. Because the "affair" occurred in Las Vegas, it was quite likely that he was from somewhere else, in town for a convention or just passing through. He never knew that she existed.

I wondered what that would be like, to find out you were pregnant by someone you barely knew and who was long gone. Did the mother think of aborting or giving the baby up for adoption? What made her decide to keep Danielle? No one but the mother would ever know that, yet Bernie and I learned a lot about her from the report, with the exception of her first name. She was simply referred to as "Mother" throughout, which seemed like a bit of a stretch to me. She was born in Syracuse, New York, and graduated from high school there. At some point, she, her mother, and her two sisters moved to Florida. She claimed to have attended three years at the University of Tampa, but no proof of her enrollment there was ever found. She also said that she obtained an AA degree in the "law" field, but the medical professionals who worked with her believe that is untrue because tests showed that she was in the borderline range of intellectual ability.

"Borderline range of intellectual ability." That raised a flag for me. What did borderline range mean, and how did that affect Danielle?

The mother had two sons from her first marriage. Thomas would have been sixteen when Danielle was born, and the second son, David, was thirteen.* The entire family moved to Florida in 2000.

It was determined that the younger son had a learning disorder, was "slow," according to his mother; in school he was put in Special Ed. Thomas was of average intelligence, although he did not finish high school. Like "Mother," they both worked part time, on and off, here and there, and received social security. David had one arrest charge, in October 2001, for alleged battery against a school bus driver.

It seemed to me that they were like thousands of families in America who eke out a living on government aid and minimum wage, occupy cheap rental housing, and rely on public transportation to get around and emergency rooms and clinics for medical care; they pay bills with cash or money orders. Because they have no

---

* The first names of Michelle Crockett's sons have been changed.

bank accounts or credit cards and own nothing of real value, they don't leave much of a paper trail. They live below the radar.

But sometimes a blip appears, which is what happened in February 2002. Before Garet read the next section, she stopped, took a drink of her water, and asked whether we wanted to take a break. Bernie glanced at his watch and said no. I sensed that something disturbing was coming. The look on Garet's face was a mixture of sadness and anger.

She took a deep breath and began the next section of the study: "Departmental History." In February 2002, an anonymous call was made to the Abuse Hotline of the Florida Department of Children and Families. The caller alleged that "Ongoing, the mother does not clean the living area and the home is filthy. The rug is dirty. There are clothes everywhere. There are feces on the child's seat in the home and the counter is covered with trash and clutter. The child is never seen dressed. She is always in a diaper or naked."

With that kind of detail, I guessed that it was someone who had been in the apartment to see the filth and the naked child, maybe a maintenance person or a property manager. Whoever made the call was trying to do the right thing and get Danielle the help she needed.

The response from the DCF was to assign the case to Child Protective Investigations. The victims in this first report were identified as David Crockett, who was sixteen at the time, and Danielle, who was three and a half. The allegations were of conditions hazardous to health and neglect.

On the initial visit, David and Danielle were at home alone. David said his mother was at work and would be home later. When the investigator was able to speak with the mother, she claimed that Danielle didn't like to wear clothing, but she forced the child to when they went outside, which she said she attempted to do at least once a week. She said that her sons attended a nearby adult school and that she did not leave for work until one of them was home to watch Danielle. She admitted that the child had no pediatrician; she insisted that Danielle's shots were up to date, but she produced no records.

On a follow-up visit about ten days later, the home was in worse disarray and smelled of cigarettes. Two days after that, on a third visit, the home had been cleaned and clothes picked up.

Ultimately, the mother was warned about smoking too much around the child. She declined the department's offer of day-care and after-school services, the risk to the child was assessed as low, and the case was closed.

Nine months later, another call was made to the DCF, this one worse than the first. The caller said that at four years old, the child was still in a diaper and drinking from a bottle and was never seen outside the home. The report alleged that the mother frequently left the younger son and Danielle at home while she worked and spent her nights with a new "paramour" in his home. I didn't think I had ever seen a boyfriend referred to as a *paramour* and wondered whether the person writing the report had a peculiar sense of humor or was just very old school.

An investigator went out the next day. According to that report, which was documented in the *Study of the Child*, Danielle had no marks or bruises and was asleep under the covers. Did the investigator uncover Danielle and make sure there were no marks or simply assume? Or just didn't bother? The boys said there was always a babysitter. Mother admitted that she did leave the children home alone once a week, but she was about to break up with her "paramour." She explained that Danielle slept in a diaper at night because she still had "accidents," although no one asked why Danielle was always in a diaper during the day. Mother also said Danielle took a bottle at night only when she "has a fit" without it. She admitted to still having no pediatrician but said she would take Danielle to the hospital if she got sick. The kitchen stove was covered in food, which the investigator pointed out would attract bugs.

Other witnesses in the apartment complex told investigators that they did not believe the mother was a "fit mother," that the child was always either naked or in a diaper, and that both Danielle and David lacked supervision.

The alleged maltreatment is again listed as Inadequate Supervisory Care Present and Inadequate Clothing and the maltreatment type as Neglect.

Again, the conclusion was that the risk was "low, based on the children are visible to the apartment community." Visible how? Through the window? It had already been reported that Danielle was never seen outside. Again, the mother refused services. Again, the case was closed due to no present indicators of inadequate supervisory care. So, adequate supervisory care was determined to be her mentally disabled adolescent brother, home alone with his defenseless, naked baby sister. Again, the DCF walked away.

By this time I was in tears. Bernie had stopped eating. The conditions Danielle had been living in were horrible, and even when people tried to help, she was left with Monster Mother. It was just inconceivable to me that a mother could have so little maternal instinct for her own child.

I worried—too much, Bernie always says—when one of my boys had a fever or a stomach ache. If they had a nightmare and cried out from their beds, I woke up and raced to comfort them. Surely, there had to have been times when Danielle had gotten sick or frightened and cried out in the night. Who took her temperature? Who held her, rocked her, whispering words of comfort until she slipped back into sleep?

I looked at Garet and asked her how the DCF could have left Danielle there, especially after the second call in less than a year. She said simply, "Someone blew it."

I thought about the children who make sensational stories on the six o'clock news when they are discovered dead, murdered at the hands of their own mothers or fathers or both. I doubt that death was the first act of abuse, but it was certainly the last.

One neighbor says to the reporter, "We had no idea." Another might admit, "The child never did look quite right." People ask, "How could this happen?" Outrage ensues, agency heads and politicians promise action, someone gets suspended while an investigation begins and then is quietly transferred to another department a few weeks later.

I had a sickening feeling that all of the children Bernie and I had looked at on the Internet who were in the foster-care system and available for adoption had been through scenarios exactly like this. No wonder they were so damaged. First, their parents let them down, and then the system that was meant to save them failed them instead.

Garet went back to reading the report. "Danielle was again brought to the attention of Children and Families through abuse report 2005–415132, which was received on July 12, 2005, at 12:34 p.m."

Bernie and I looked at each other, then at Garet. That was three years between calls. What had happened to the poor child during that time?

7

Nowhere Child

The next part of the *Study of the Child* explained in nauseating detail how it was that Danielle finally came into state custody. It amazed Bernie and me how extreme conditions had to be for the DCF to finally say, "Enough."

The third complaint was pretty much like the ones taken three years earlier. A call to the hotline came in at 12:34 p.m. on July 12, 2005. It charged that the mother regularly left Danielle under her brother David's supervision, that she was still wearing diapers and was not potty-trained, that she cried or mumbled but was otherwise nonverbal, that she might be mentally handicapped, and that David was certainly mentally handicapped.

Once again, I thought that whoever made that call had to have been in the house to have seen her. Could it have been another "paramour" of the mother's? A girlfriend of one of the sons? Were they still living in the same apartment complex? Everything in the report raised more questions for me than it answered.

The day after the call, a DCF investigator and a police car were sent to the house and met there. As Garet continued reading, I was skimming over the same words. It was so much worse than the first two times the DCF had come to investigate. Danielle was found sleeping in a filthy bedroom that contained old soiled mattresses. The floor was covered in trash and dirty diapers. There were countless cockroaches and spiders. The child was extremely thin, with ribs poking from her body. She was dirty, with matted hair, numerous bug bites all over her body, and scratches. She was dressed only in a wet diaper and was nonverbal, only grunting or crying.

The mother stated that the daughter was mentally delayed in some capacity, but she had never taken her to a doctor to get a diagnosis, nor did she have a pediatrician or take her daughter for medical attention. The child was not on Medicaid and, according to the mother, was denied for Florida Kidcare.

Florida Kidcare is a program that provides health insurance for children between birth and age eighteen. There's a fairly extensive application to be filled out and a lengthy review process. I couldn't imagine why Danielle would have been denied. More likely, her mother never applied because she didn't want to do anything that would bring attention to her daughter or the conditions under which she was living.

The mother claimed that the daughter ate all of the time and that she especially liked to eat canned pasta, like ravioli. She also said that she bathed her daughter about four times a week.

The rest of the house was observed to be in "deplorable condition." There were cats and a dog roaming freely and animal feces. Roaches were crawling on the dishes, the walls, and the floor of the kitchen. The refrigerator had food but also dead roaches in the drawers and inside the door of the freezer. "It appeared that the house was infested with roaches. The house appeared to have not been cleaned in some time and smelled of cigarette smoke and cat urine."

From there, the report jumped to Danielle being seen by the Child Protective Team "due to concern regarding her delays and numerous bug bites."

I stopped Garet to clarify. Where was she seen and when? Garet had a lot more information on the case and on Danielle than was chronicled in the *Child Study*. She told us that Detective Mark Holste had made the call from the Plant City Police Department. He and his partner first saw the DCF employee standing by her car in the yard, crying. She had gone inside to find the child and told the officers that it was the worst case she had ever seen. They went into the house to question the mother and see the little girl. It was Detective Holste who carried Danielle out of the house and told the DCF worker to let her supervisor know she would be taking Danielle to the hospital.

Garet said that police photographs used as evidence in the hearing showed a clapboard shack, dingy and mud-spattered, with peeling paint and a rusted tin roof. Inside was a tiny living room with broken-down furniture and a carpet so covered with roaches, dead and alive, that it actually crunched under Detective Holste's shoes. Everywhere he looked, ashtrays were overflowing with cigarette butts, with more crushed out on the floor. The kitchen and the bathroom were vile—more dead cockroaches, food-encrusted dishes, greasy pans, a cat litter box and feces, and black mold over every surface of the bathroom.

But it was the photos of Danielle's room that Garet said horrified everyone the most. The room was in the rear of the house, dark, with one window boarded up, and the other broken in half, the jagged edge of glass halfway up the frame. On the floor was the bare mattress where Danielle spent her days and nights—soiled, stained, moldy, its sides ripped open, stuffing and springs popping out onto the floor. Piles of clothes and mounds of trash were on another mattress overlapping the one Danielle lived on. Except for a table with a small television, there was no other furniture in the tiny room, which was smaller than a walk-in closet.

When Detective Holste took Danielle from the home, she was wearing only a dripping diaper, and the clothing in the house was so moldy and dirty, it couldn't be worn. He wrapped her up in a blanket, got her one of the stuffed animals he kept in the squad car trunk to comfort frightened children, and sent her to the hospital with the social worker.

In my mind, I was seeing Detective Holste as the action hero who swooped in and rescued Danielle from the evil stepmother, the deplorable house, the cockroach colony, the bug bites and scratches, the cat urine and dog feces, the cigarette smoke, the matted hair infested with lice, the lack of clothing, toys, and decent food. Danielle was a nearly seven-year-old speechless child, clothed only in a dirty diaper and hidden away in a filthy bedroom on a soiled mattress.

It took all of that misery, Detective Holste, and whoever placed that last call to the hotline before an appropriate response was made and Danielle was taken out of the hellhole she had endured for almost seven years.

This mother's utter indifference to her daughter's well-being and her skill at scamming the system merged with the complete dysfunction of Florida's DCF and nearly resulted in another story about a child falling through the cracks and turning up dead.

I didn't believe Danielle fell through the cracks. She was pushed—by her mother, by her brothers, and by the agency charged with protecting children. For the first seven years of her life, Danielle existed nowhere but in her own world. It had to have been better than the world her mother imprisoned her in.

8

Into the System

We were on page eight of the *Child Study*, which was fourteen pages in all. I had lost my appetite altogether. I excused myself to go the restroom and get a little break.

I splashed some water on my face and looked in the mirror over the sink. It occurred to me that if we were able to adopt Danielle, she would be the only person in our house with brown eyes. Bernie, William, and I all have blue eyes. My boys Paul and Steven have blue eyes.

I had to laugh at myself. Of all the things we would confront if we were able to do this, all of the obstacles and challenges, I was worried about Danielle feeling left out of our family because she didn't have blue eyes? I dried my face, took a deep breath, and went back to the table.

Bernie and Garet were chatting like old friends, which is Bernie's way. He makes personal connections quickly and naturally, whether it's with the paint guy at Lowe's, the checkout woman at the grocery store, the new preacher at church, or a little girl sitting in a swing, deep in her own world. Bernie would make a great Wal-Mart greeter, except that he wouldn't be content with simply welcoming shoppers and answering questions; he would have to walk the person back to the small appliance department, help her pick out the best blender, coffeemaker, and electric frying pan, then push her buggy back to the checkout line while asking how old her children were and where they went to school.

Bernie was grilling Garet—in the nicest possible way—on how she came to be involved in the case. He wanted more details: where was she when she first saw Danielle, what did Danielle do, what did Garet do, was Danielle afraid, did she cry? Had Garet met Detective Holste? Could we meet Detective Holste? How did Danielle's picture come to be in the Heart Gallery? When could we take her home with us? He sounded just like Willie on the phone. Like father, like son. These were the same questions I had, but I also knew we needed to get back to Fort Myers Beach, or Willie would stay up all night waiting for us.

Garet looked a bit overwhelmed, which I took as my cue to pick up our copy of the report and ask, "Where were we?"

She resumed reading on page eight, and we tracked through a synopsis of the legal proceedings that had taken place since Danielle was removed from the home on July 13, 2005. A shelter hearing was held the next day, which Garet said is required by law to take place within twenty-four hours. The shelter petition was granted, and a guardian ad litem—a person who has the legal authority to care for the personal interests of another person—was assigned to the case. For the first time in her life, Danielle would have an adult advocating for her. I murmured a prayer of thanks for the guardian ad litem program.

Along with the guardian ad litem, Danielle was appointed an attorney ad litem to execute all of the legal proceedings that were ahead of her.

Most important in my mind, July 14 was the day that Garet first encountered the case, because she happened to be in the courtroom on another matter and had stayed with some other agency workers to listen in on the case everyone was whispering about.

At the next hearing on August 9, the judge ordered that Danielle be tested for hearing, speech, and disability and that a comprehensive assessment be completed. The judge also ordered that the mother have no visitation with the child until further order of the court. I almost spit my coffee across the table; it seemed ridiculous that there would be any possibility of allowing the woman within a hundred yards of Danielle.

On September 27, Hillsborough Kids Inc. (HKI) and the attorney general filed a Petition for Expedited Termination of Parental Rights. Garet explained to us that this meant that HKI would not file a case plan, which is required if the parties are working for reunification of the family. No one, Garet assured us, thought reunification of Danielle with her mother and brothers was feasible.

The advisory hearing was scheduled for November 3, then rescheduled for November 6, and the trial date was set for February 2006 to allow time for the mother to be assessed by a therapist.

I felt a shudder of revulsion to see the last paragraph on the page. It consisted of words copied verbatim from a handwritten letter the mother had mailed to the North Care Center on March 23.

To Whom It May Concern: My daughter Danielle is a young beautiful lady. I care for her for 6 years until you took her away from me. She was never abuse by any family member. She was love and care for. She was well feed and happy and healthy. I used to read to her, take her to the park, take her shopping with me, take her to the library. My house became a rundown do to I just started my new job and I was sick for 3 months with bronchitis. I have my life straight out now and I need to get my daughter back. She is the love of my life

and I cry everyday for Danielle. Please let me see her again.
I need to know she is okay or hear her on the phone. Thank
you, [mother].

Bernie looked at Garet and said exactly what I was thinking.
"What world is that woman living in? How can she think anyone
would believe her?"

Luckily, the courts did not believe her. I'm sure it wasn't the
first time that someone who was about to lose her child through
her own actions had lied. The Termination of Parental Rights Trial
was held from August 21 through August 26. The mother, her boys,
the Plant City Police Department, HKI, the guardian ad litem, and
Dr. Kathleen Armstrong all gave testimony.

The Petition for Termination of Parental Rights was accepted
after the trial, and Judge Martha Cook entered a sixteen-page
Order of Adjudication of Dependency and Judgment of Involuntary
Termination of Parental Rights as to the mother and the father on
September 21, 2006. I imagined a gavel coming down on a block of
wood as she pronounced the decision.

The date rang a bell in my head. I turned back to the cover
page of the report. Just under her name, Danielle Ann Crockett,
and beside her photo was "Child's Date of Birth: September 21st,
1998." Below that: "Date of Adjudication: September 21, 2006."
I showed Bernie, and tears came to his eyes as they had to mine.
I'm sure it was a coincidence that Danielle was emancipated on her
eighth birthday. But we took it as a sign that God was sending his
precious child the most beautiful gift, clearing the way for her new
life to begin.

9

Truth and Consequences

The termination of parental rights had legally freed Danielle from her mother on her eighth birthday, but this didn't mean that Danielle would ever be free of the heart-wrenching consequences of being under that woman's control for the first seven years of her life.

The next part of the *Child Study* was titled "Medical & Developmental Information." I felt my stomach turn and my throat tighten again; we were about to hear the hard facts about Danielle's physical and intellectual state from the time she was taken into custody up until the present. We had already witnessed some of her behavioral and developmental issues that day.

The first people to test Danielle were members of the Child Protection Team at Tampa General Hospital shortly after she was removed from her home. As big a step as it was toward getting her well physically, she must have been so frightened. After being taken from the only environment she had ever known, surrounded by the only people she had ever known, where she had been left alone in a dim and dirty room, day and night, Danielle was transported to the brightly lit, ultrasanitized, loud, bustling environment of a children's hospital. She was being bathed, changed, and examined by complete strangers, eating unfamiliar food, and sleeping in an unfamiliar bed. Garet told us that she had been placed in an oversized crib, with bars that reached higher than she could climb. I thought she must have been, at the least, confused and disoriented, if not terrified, and I felt so sad for her.

Whether Danielle knew it or could express it, all that she probably wanted was to be held on someone's lap like a child with her mother, safe, secure, and loved. Instead, she was being poked, prodded, and tested. I hoped that during the testing and the observation, someone took a moment to give her a hug, stroke her hair, kiss her forehead, hold her hand, and whisper reassurances in her ear.

She certainly needed them. "Aggressive, self-mutilating and repetitive behaviors were noted by staff." She had reduced eye contact. She was not potty-trained, although she was six years and nine months old. Her lungs, heart, hands, feet, and nails were normal. There was no scoliosis. There were bruises and insect bites on her extremities. The doctor noted subtle dysmorphia, as well as macrocephaly with a broad forehead and apparent hypertolorism. I wasn't sure how to pronounce those terms, much less what they meant.

But Garet had done her homework and had made notes on her copy of the *Child Study.* I did the same on mine, though I intended to look the terms up on the Internet when we were back home.

Dysmorphia is an unrealistic body image, like when thin girls truly see themselves as fat and starve themselves over it. We didn't know how Danielle could express anything like that to a doctor, but

Garet thought maybe it meant that Danielle perceived herself to be smaller than she was.

Macrocephaly occurs when the head is abnormally large, and hypertolorism is an abnormal distance between two organs or body parts, frequently the eyes. Maybe I hadn't been looking closely enough at Danielle's head when we were with her, but it didn't seem very big to me, and although her eyes were wide set, they did not seem abnormally so. On our way to meet Garet at the restaurant, Bernie and I talked about how pretty Danielle was, much more than we anticipated from the original picture we had seen through the Heart Gallery.

The doctor requested more testing—chromosomal, fragile X DNA, and genetic. He noted that although Danielle's developmental and behavioral difficulties appeared to have some familial basis, he believed that much of her delay was based on environmental neglect. Developmental pediatricians also assessed Danielle and felt that her development on a physical level—gross and fine motor skills—as well as her speech and socialization, was delayed to approximately the four- to six-month level.

That was a blow. I tried to remember what a four-month-old does, but it had been years since I'd had one, and a child's first year goes so fast, you barely have time to write one milestone in the Baby's First Year book before another one happens. There had been few milestones to mark in Danielle's life, and I'm sure no one would find a Baby's First Year journal in her house.

The mother was also questioned by the same team. She told them that Danielle had never talked, could not feed herself, and had never been to see a doctor. Never? I couldn't fathom it. I had always been so compulsive about checkups and immunizations. I kept all of the boys' medical reports in folders, along with notes on sick visits and the occasional trip to the ER that is as much a part of raising kids as coloring on the walls and juice stains on the sofa.

Our boys were healthy and reached developmental markers at the appropriate ages. How could this woman not take her daughter to a doctor when she wasn't speaking at two years old? Didn't Danielle ever once get sick? Have a sore throat, an ear infection, or an upset stomach? Yet the mother told the examiner that she had no concerns about her daughter's health.

The mother admitted that she kept the child inside because she was afraid that she—the mother—would get in trouble because the child was not ready for school. She said that Danielle walked at one and a half years and could say three to four words, including *mom*, *love*, and *bro*.

Garet looked at us and shook her head. It seemed to me that if Danielle had been speaking, she would have spoken to Garet, Mr. O'Keefe, or Ms. Perez, and so far, she had not.

The mother later contradicted her earlier statements and said that Danielle could feed herself, although her diet consisted mainly of finger foods, canned pasta such as ravioli (which I assumed she picked up with her fingers), and anything she was able to drink from her sippy cup.

In late July, while still in the hospital, Danielle was also evaluated by Dr. Kathleen Armstrong, the director of the Health Pediatric Psychology Program at the University of South Florida (USF). It was Garet who took Danielle to those appointments. Garet told us that normally they would get an assessment from a myriad of doctors, but Dr. Armstrong is a nationally recognized expert in severe trauma, and she was recommended by Tampa General.

Garet drove Danielle to USF and walked with her to Dr. Armstrong's building, holding her hand so that she wouldn't bolt, which was one of her favorite things to do. It was easy to gain access to the break area from the waiting room, so Danielle went in there and walked around banging on soda machines, rearranging chairs, and was just constantly moving. One of Dr. Armstrong's staff was eating lunch in the break room, and she had some cold chicken on a plate. Danielle walked over to her, grabbed a chicken leg, put it in her mouth, and looked at Garet, then at the lady. The lady got so mad. She told Garet, "Get your daughter away from my lunch." The thing with Danielle, Garet explained, was that unless you looked really closely or she was having a fit, she didn't appear to be obviously handicapped. Although she was on medication that caused her to drool and her tongue to hang out the side of her mouth when she was tired, she didn't look like a Down syndrome child, and she wasn't in a wheelchair. She could be mistaken for a very ill-behaved little girl—which is probably what this woman assumed. You wouldn't think the lady would want the chicken after it was in Danielle's mouth, but she did. So Garet tugged the chicken leg out of Danielle's mouth, washed it off, and laid it back on the woman's plate.

Bernie was laughing so hard at the story that he nearly choked, and I think I smiled for the first time since we had sat down with the report. We could both visualize Danielle with a chicken leg in her mouth, probably looking like one of our dogs when it takes something it knows it is not supposed to have.

The moment of humor was brief, because the information on the next few pages was devastating.

Dr. Armstrong's report included observations from the hospital, as well as input from Garet. Danielle was reported to be eating like an infant, tolerating a bottle with milk and some table foods, which had to be fed to her. Her sleep habits were often disrupted, although she napped two times a day for thirty to sixty minutes. That sounded like a plus to me. My kids' naps were my favorite time of the day, and my boys stopped taking them long before I was ready to give up this quiet break.

Danielle was described to Dr. Armstrong as a little girl who kept to herself and did not initiate contact. In the hospital, she initially exhibited self-stimulatory behaviors, including head banging, head shaking from side to side, hand flapping, aversion of gaze, and rocking and pulling away from attempts at contact. After several days, the hospital staff said that she was making brief eye contact and would allow hugs. But "she roams about the hospital floor or playroom without purpose. She does not use a crayon or a spoon. She does not stack blocks. She does not help with dressing or use a cup.

"Danielle laughs and occasionally uses babbling sounds, but is usually silent. She does not follow one step commands."

The next section was a combination of two different testing methods to measure where Danielle was in certain abilities and functions. It was eye-opening, to say the least.

Gross Motor	20 months
Visual Reception	4 months
Fine Motor	9 months
Receptive Language	2 months
Expressive Language	6 months
Physical Age	20 months
Self Help Age	6 months
Social Age	4 months
Academic Age	6 months
Communication Age	2 months

I wondered whether my face looked like Bernie's—a combination of shock, sadness, and anger. I felt like we were being pummeled, and the blows kept coming.

Danielle's next evaluation was done nearly a year after she had been removed from custody. She had been living in the Medical Foster Home for nine months, had been in Mr. O'Keefe's classroom for about seven months, and was nearly eight years old. Even so, it was more of the same. "She will start crying and screaming for no reason. She is not able to feed herself. She is not able to speak. She walks on her tippy toes. Her cognitive function, communication, social and emotional interaction and self-help skills are severely delayed. She moves about the room with her own stimuli. She makes sounds that are similar to an airplane."

And yet—I knew I was desperately seeking just a shard of hope—"Danielle will briefly focus on faces and does seem to discriminate against strangers. It appears she is beginning to show some object permanence. She typically puts toys in her mouth but makes no attempt to eat them. There was what appears to be some autism, though no active hallucinations or delusions. She does not appear to be psychotic. She is not verbal in any domain and does not appear to have the skills necessary to speak, although her caseworker did note that she is able to say a few words." That sounded positive to me, and I could see Bernie's face relaxing a tiny bit.

And in the next section, which was educational information dated November 2006—the start of Danielle's second year in Mr. O'Keefe's room—she was described as a "happy, active and affectionate child." I could tell after spending even just a little time with Mr. O'Keefe that those were his words. I sensed that he was a man of great faith and empathy, who believed that anything was possible. He explained her limitations and challenges, but he did it in a positive and loving way.

"She enjoys repetitive movements with toys and other objects found in the classroom. She also likes to use voice output devices and vocal toys to make noises. Danielle is unable to stay seated during mealtime but she will stay seated in a chair with very close adult proximity and verbal encouragement. She can run and climb. . . . Danielle has infrequent crying episodes where she becomes very agitated. . . . Socially, she smiles often, makes fleeting eye contact and shows recognition of caregivers. . . . She seems to feel comfortable among her peers in most of the school environments she is exposed to. . . . She indicates her feelings through vocalizations such as crying and laughing."

That was the good news, and I was very grateful for any tiny morsel of hope.

"As a result of Danielle's disability, her cognitive skills are below what is required for success in the general curriculum with modifications. She requires continuous supervision to prevent her from getting into a dangerous situation, such as climbing or running toward danger. . . . She requires assistance for participation in all classroom activities, social skills and daily living skills. . . . Danielle's expressive and receptive communication skills are severely delayed. She has limited understanding of basic vocabulary. She has difficulty carrying out directions from others, attending to an activity and indicating choices."

The words on the paper were swimming in front of me, and I realized it was because tears were falling from my eyes onto the paper. The whole day had been an emotional roller coaster. The excitement about meeting Danielle, the other children in her classroom, her fiendish behavior, Bernie's immediate connection with her, my uneasiness while changing her diaper, and our relief that she had people like Mr. O'Keefe, Ms. Perez, and especially Garet the Angel watching over her. Then fourteen grueling pages of the good, the very bad, and the hideously ugly.

What really had hit me hardest in the report was hearing about the two previous times the DCF had been called to the house and had left her there. Aside from the obvious—to anyone but the DCF, I guess—neglect, I wondered whether Danielle had experienced something while she was wandering nearly naked and defenseless, under the "care" of her developmentally disabled brother.

What would have been different had the DCF taken Danielle into care when she was only three or had just turned four? What if, at the very least, the mother had been required to take parenting classes or take her daughter to a doctor or to speech therapy?

Instead, Danielle spent three more years with no medical care or education. For three more years she was denied love, affection, security, protection, comfort, teddy bears, hugs, lullabies, bedtime stories, good morning kisses, the feeling of sunshine on her face, and the sound of birds singing.

I couldn't imagine how she had survived it. Reading the *Child Study* and hearing the things that Garet told us to fill in the blanks, we were amazed that Danielle had lived long enough to ever have her picture on the wall that day at GameWorks.

Seeing how much Garet loved Danielle, how Mr. O'Keefe and Ms. Perez cared for her, and hearing about Detective Holste, I began to believe that we were part of some bigger plan. I had read stories of the babies in the Romanian orphanages who ultimately died from lack of human contact. At the very least, those children were changed, bathed, and fed, but they were not given love, affection, attention, or hope, and they simply withered away. Danielle had experienced none of those things, but somehow she held on. For what? For us?

10

Butterflies Are Free

The last page of the report was a signature page, with the name of the person who wrote it; that of Garet White, showing that she had reviewed and accepted it; that of her supervisor; her supervisor's supervisor, and finally "Potential Adoptive Mother" and "Potential Adoptive Father."

At that point, we could have decided not to sign it. We could have paid the check for lunch, thanked Garet for her time, wished her well in finding a home for Danielle, and driven back to our peaceful, orderly home in which resided one well-behaved and fairly quiet young man, three little house-trained dogs, and a lazy cat that awoke only to move with the sun and come into the house at night. No one would have thought badly of us or judged us.

When we first met Garet at her office before we went to the school, she told us that under normal circumstances, the procedure was for her to read the *Child Study* to "potential" parents while recording it for them, give them their copy, and get their signatures before they met the child.

But Garet knew these circumstances weren't quite normal, to say the least. So she spoke to her supervisors, who agreed that it would be in our best interests, as well as Danielle's, for us to meet Danielle up front, given all of her special needs and challenges. They thought it was impossible to explain on paper the struggles that Danielle was dealing with and that it was important for any family to meet and observe her before moving ahead in the process. They felt that Danielle would not be aware that we were interested in adopting her, so she would be none the wiser if we decided that she was more than we could handle. She would never know if, after meeting her, we decided not to follow through with adoption. We would just be two more people who came and went in her life.

Bernie and I looked at each other across the table and reached for the pen at the same time. Ever the gentleman, he let me sign first. In reality, we knew that signing the papers didn't mean we had to go through with it, just as we knew that the signed papers' calling us potential parents didn't mean we were guaranteed to get Danielle. It was more like we were now committed to the next steps, and time would tell what might happen. But still, chill bumps came up on my arms as we signed our names, and looking at Bernie, I was afraid he was going to high-five me.

As we gathered up the paperwork, Garet suggested that we read the *Child Study* again and do some research on the Internet about brain development and speech development in children. She said we had seventy-two hours to make up our minds if we wanted another visit with Danielle, but legally we had to wait twenty-four hours to notify them either way. Bernie and I both looked at our watches. It was 4:05 p.m.

We practically ran to the parking lot to get in the car. Rush-hour traffic around Tampa is a migraine in waiting. We were eager to get back to Fort Myers Beach, sit on our deck, and watch the sunset.

We talked all the way home in the car—about Danielle, about Ms. Perez and Mr. O'Keefe, about Detective Holste and the Florida DCF. Whether it was incompetence or indifference, the DCF had, as Garet said, blown it. I asked Bernie what he and Garet had talked about while I was in the restroom collecting myself. He had asked her how she came to work in this field and how she had met Danielle. If the Wal-Mart greeter thing doesn't pan out for him, he could be an investigator of some kind. He is so good at getting people to open up about themselves. He can be so disarming and ingratiating that before you are even aware of it, he has sucked you right in.

It turned out that Garet was adopted. She told Bernie she had always known. She even met her birth mother when she was older and had a good relationship with this woman, but Garet considers her parents to be the people who raised her. Garet was from Cleveland but was enrolled in boarding schools in Bell Buckle, Tennessee, and then in Philadelphia. After high school, she went to Boston College, then floated back and forth between New York and Los Angeles to try to break into acting. That surprised me a little bit. She was so reserved. I couldn't imagine her getting up on stage as the center of attention.

Garet eventually went back to college to study sociology and psychology and, after getting her degree, did social work in various areas, but when she had her son six years ago, she felt a calling to work with kids who had issues. Which is how she ended up with one of the three private agencies under the umbrella of Hillsborough Kids, Inc. HKI took over many of the duties of the DCF, after some highly publicized incidents involving children who had become lost in that system. All the DCF was supposed to do was investigate reports of abuse or neglect, determine the validity of the reports, and then turn everything over to the police and the private agencies. Considering how the DCF blew it with Danielle, I was surprised it was still allowed to do that much.

If Garet wanted to work with kids who had issues, she found a bottomless pool of them in child protective services and the foster care system. There aren't many children more prone to having issues than kids who have been physically, sexually, or emotionally abused by their parents; neglected like Danielle; or abandoned altogether.

Garet told Bernie that she just happened to be in the courtroom on the day of the shelter hearing for Danielle, which was the day after Danielle had been taken to Tampa General. Everybody had been whispering about the case, the condition of the house, the condition of the child. The police had taken photos to be entered into evidence as proof that Danielle needed to be sheltered. The hearing Garet was attending had finished, but she decided to stay to see what would happen to this girl. The DCF described the condition of the house and the child, and everyone was aghast. Garet asked the bailiff to ask the judge which care center Danielle would be assigned to, and, as it turned out, it was the one where Garet worked. Garet asked the judge whether she could have the case, if her supervisor okayed it, which apparently was not the way things were supposed to proceed, and Garet was definitely not following protocol. But she told Bernie that for whatever reason, she was drawn to this little girl whom she still hadn't met. Garet called her supervisor, who called his supervisor and got the okay, but Garet ended up getting a reprimand from her agency and the DCF. As Bernie told me all of this, I said a silent prayer of thanks to Garet. If she had not risked pissing off her supervisors and the DCF, who knows where Danielle might have ended up?

From the courtroom, Garet went straight to the hospital and found Danielle at the nurse's station in one of the little wagons they keep in the children's hospital. A nurse was feeding her chocolate pudding, and it was all over her mouth. The situation was pretty overwhelming for the staff. They have a lot of sick patients to care for, and then they get this little girl who can't speak, can't feed herself, isn't potty-trained, and is making animal noises and throwing herself around. Under the bug bites, the ratted hair, the pale skin, and the sunken eyes, you could see that Danielle was a pretty girl, but Garet told Bernie that it was like there was no one inside her. She looked right through everyone around her as if she didn't see them.

After Garet showed the nurses her ID, she asked if she could take Danielle for a walk. They practically shouted, "Yes!" So Garet pulled the wagon with Danielle through the halls of the hospital. The theme of the children's hospital is fish—they're painted on the walls and on the floors, and there are live fish in big aquariums. Garet stopped and pointed out the fish to Danielle, but she didn't seem to especially notice or like them.

I wondered what Danielle had been thinking, whether anything was registering. She had been indoors for years. She had never been to the beach or seen fish. She had never visited the park. She had never been taken outside of her house for any reason, except to move from Las Vegas to Florida and then from one crummy rental to another.

Garet pulled the wagon to a big picture of butterflies. She pointed to them and told Danielle, "These are butterflies, they are beautiful, like you. They fly around outside in the sun, just like you will one day."

Bernie stopped talking. I looked at him, and he was choked up. I touched his arm and asked him what had happened. He said that Garet told him that after she showed Danielle the butterflies, Danielle reached up from the wagon toward Garet to be picked up. Garet held her up to the picture, and Danielle stretched out her hand, gently patted the butterflies painted on the wall, and smiled. Bernie said this was the moment that Garet knew there was a little girl inside, and she made a promise to Danielle that she would do anything and everything she could to find a family who wanted to take Danielle home, who would give her the care and love she had never had.

Garet told Bernie that no one else in the adoption unit thought Danielle could be adopted, but Garet always had a feeling that Danielle would find a home somewhere. She believed that there was a better place waiting for Danielle. Garet knew it would be tough, but she didn't think it would be impossible.

Bernie laughed. Garet admitted to him that she never thought she'd find that family in a GameWorks arcade or that the initial connection would be made through the terrible photo taken on the day Danielle was admitted to the hospital. All of the social workers and the Heart Gallery people on duty that day thought we were a little bit delusional.

Besides the *Child Study*, Garet had also given us copies of legal documents from the time of the shelter hearing to that of the Termination of Parental Rights and up to the present, as well as copies of the medical reports and evaluations for Danielle, her mother, and the boys from which the *Child Study* was written. There were thick black lines drawn through the mother's name; we assumed her last name was the same as Danielle's but couldn't be sure.

There was a copy of the most recent abuse report, the one that resulted in Danielle's removal, and photocopies of the photographs the police department took of the house on the day Danielle was removed. At that point, my mental and emotional in-box was overflowing, and all I wanted was to go home and see Willie.

I turned back to Bernie, who was replaying the classroom visit out loud, with as much enthusiasm as if we had been to a grade school pageant or field day. He was thrilled about the connection he had made with Danielle through the swing and the Slinky, and he was convinced that she had connected with him, too. "Diane, she made eye contact with me! They said she had never done that with a stranger before. They were crying over it! It was incredible."

If he believed that she had connected with him, then I believed it, too. I was glad to see him so excited—he had certainly come a long way since telling me I was crazy for wanting to bring another child into our home. Hello, pot, kettle speaking. At this point, he was possibly crazier than me.

I was the pragmatic one in our marriage. I needed to form a realistic picture of how bringing this little girl into our home would affect our family, especially Willie, who had been sold on the idea of adoption, thinking that he would have a playmate. How much of a playmate would or could Danielle ever be? She would need an extraordinary amount of attention, which would mean less attention for Willie He was a sweet-natured, compassionate, patient, incredibly generous and nurturing child, but would Danielle be such a burden that he would come to resent her?

We could not possibly make a decision about the impact on Willie without his input. How he felt about it would be key, so he had to be nearly as informed as we were. There would be things that would be tough for a nine-year-old boy to hear and almost impossible to understand. Willie had never known anything but love from everyone around him. How could he possibly comprehend what happens to a little girl who has never known love at all?

It was dark, close to his bedtime, when we picked him up from Evie's house. After giving Willie a short version of the day, promising to elaborate at dinner the next night, and settling him in, Bernie and I both fell into bed, but only one of us fell asleep. I stared at the ceiling, then at the clock beside the bed, and then the ceiling again, hoping that the whirling blades of the ceiling fan might do the trick. But my mind was racing, and I was curious about what was in the other papers Garet had given us. Finally, about 3 a.m., two hours before I normally get up, I figured that as long as my brain was so busy, I might as well put it to good use. I got out of bed, went to the kitchen, started some coffee, got the folders, and sat down at the kitchen table.

The court papers were long and laborious to slog through, and we already knew the results of the hearing from what was included in the *Study of the Child*. I skimmed through them quickly but stopped when I saw for the first time the mother's name: Michelle Crockett. Michelle was such a pretty name for such a monstrous woman.

I read on and found that sometime between the Expedited Petition filed a year earlier and the event at the Heart Gallery, Garet had changed jobs from case worker to adoption case manager. It really turned out to be the best of all worlds for Danielle. Garet was by Danielle's side to navigate the first steps through the hospital, the exams, testing, and the Expedited TPR and get her into foster care when she first came into the system. Once Danielle was at least safe in the foster home, Garet then devoted herself to finding a family for the little girl.

The police photos were in their own envelope, and I steeled myself before I pulled them out, but nothing could have prepared me for what they showed. I turned them over, closed my eyes, and rested my forehead on my palms, pressing hard as if that would make the images go away. Bernie came into the kitchen and put his hand on my shoulder. He picked up a copy of a picture, gasped, and turned it back over. "Diane, she isn't there anymore. That's in her past. She will never go back there again, and her mother will never have control over her again. She is safe from her." I knew this, but Danielle had lived seven years in that hell, with a monster for a mother. What was that going to mean long term? Would Danielle ever recover? Was being safe enough? What about love and kisses and hugs, baby dolls and puppies, Christmas and the Easter Bunny?

I heard Willie's bedroom door open, followed by the bathroom door closing. I put the folders aside and started to make breakfast, feeling as if I were on autopilot. An hour later, Bernie threw me a kiss and a "Love you" on his way out the door. I yelled for Willie to hurry, the bus was coming. Waiting outside with him at the corner, watching him play with our dogs, I tried to picture Danielle doing the same. Maybe I was crazy, but it wasn't impossible to imagine, not after seeing the way she responded to Bernie. The bus lumbered up to the stop, Willie scrambled on and stuck his hand out the top of the window to wave good-bye. I waved back, smiled at his grinning face, and as the bus went in one direction and the dogs and I in another for our morning walk through the neighborhood, I wondered what a day with Danielle might look like.

11

All in Good Time

We moved to Florida in the fall of 2002, happy to flee another cold, wet, and dreary Tennessee winter. We loved that Fort Myers Beach was on an island—the seven-mile-long Estero Island in the southern Gulf Coast of Florida. Accessible by a four-lane bridge at the north end and a two-lane bridge on the south, it made us feel removed and secluded. Though it was a popular tourist destination, it wasn't glitzy, flashy, or fancy like Miami or filled with bars and spring breakers like Panama City Beach.

It had that Old Florida charm of cottages, screened porches, ceiling fans, slamming screen doors, clean beaches, narrow roads dusted with sand, and small mom-and-pop businesses. If visitors wanted luxury, they could find it, but people who came to Fort Myers Beach were typically looking for a quiet, low-key family vacation.

We felt like we were on family vacation all year. The weather was almost always sunny and warm. The bay was on one side of the island and the Gulf on the other, so close we could walk to either one. There were several parks close by with playgrounds that Willie loved. It was five minutes to great seafood restaurants, and there was always some fun festival or art show in one of the beach communities. The boys loved to skim board and Jet Ski. We spent most of our waking hours outdoors.

When we first moved to Florida, Paul was a junior, Steven was in middle school, and Willie was almost three. We liked the schools, and there was plenty of part-time work for the older boys after school and on weekends.

I didn't think of Laguna Shores as a subdivision but as a neighborhood. It was small, with a mix of older and newer homes, big and small, all with tidy lawns of grass or pebbles, gorgeous tropical flowers, towering palm trees, and citrus, mango, and banana trees. We could literally pick our own fruit salad fresh every day. Residents had pride in their homes and in the community and watched out for one another. It was the kind of place where everyone greeted their neighbors by name. It was safe for the boys to ride their bikes and scooters on the streets, which had as many golf carts as they did cars.

There were no over-the-top houses, although a couple of fairly well-known celebrities had second homes there. They weren't treated any differently from anyone else, which was part of the appeal. No one really paid any attention to them unless their yards got overgrown or papers piled up.

Mostly, it was retired older transplants from the north, snowbirds, which suited Bernie and me just fine. I have always been comfortable around older people, and Bernie missed his parents—who were still living in California—terribly. He was able to lend our neighbors a hand when they needed a fence fixed or a shelf put up on the wall. Paul, Steven, and Willie had their pick of nanas and papas who were all too happy to treat them as their own.

We became close to two couples in particular. The first house we bought was just down the street from Dorothy and Paul LaPiccola, who had moved to Florida from Michigan. I met Dorothy while out walking the dogs. She was like the mayor of Laguna Shores—she knew everyone and everyone's business and on any given day was taking in mail and feeding pets for at least a half dozen neighbors when they were out of town. She was gregarious, opinionated, and in charge, the kind of person you'd describe as a real pistol, and I was immediately drawn to her. Paul was quieter and easy-going, happy to sit on the sofa and watch whatever game or sporting event was on ESPN or work jigsaw puzzles. There was always a puzzle in some stage of assembly on the table.

She and Paul had a grown daughter, who had blessed them with five grandchildren. They all still lived in Michigan, which explained her attachment to Bernie, me, and our boys. They also doted on their dog, Amber, who had her own bedroom with a full-size human bed. Dorothy cooked Amber chicken breasts for dinner every night.

Our other set of surrogate parents/grandparents were Doris and Bill Kenny from Pennsylvania; of the two, Bill was the more outgoing.

About two years after we moved to Florida, the house across the street from the Kennys came up for sale, which Dorothy knew before anyone else and told us to get on it right away. As much as I know she would have liked us to stay in her sight, the other house was on the bay, and it was an opportunity to live directly on the water that we couldn't pass up. We could see the bay from our second-floor deck, and our own dock was less than fifty feet away through the backyard. There was a beautiful screened-in pool and a hot tub.

Bill was so excited, I thought he was going to start moving our furniture in by himself. He told Bernie that it wasn't often you got to pick your own neighbors, and he wasn't going to let just anybody move so close by.

The dogs and I were barely a block down the street on our walk when we ran into Dorothy, out on her morning rounds of dog, cat, and bird feeding and newspaper gathering. She peppered me with questions about the visit to the school and what we had found out.

She, Paul, Bill, and Doris had known for a long time that we were thinking of adopting, and of the four, Dorothy was the most taken aback. In fact, she told us she thought we were "out of your cotton-picking brains!" She and Paul both pointed out to us that we were on top of the world. Our Paul had graduated and moved out, Steven was close to it, William was in school, and we had our dream house with the pool.

Before we went to see Danielle for the first time, Dorothy pleaded with me not to do it. I reminded her that she and Paul had adopted their daughter, and she countered with the fact that Gayle was a perfectly healthy seven-year-old girl when she came to them.

After we saw Danielle, I gave Dorothy the highlights of the visit—Danielle's playing with Bernie, how wonderful Garet, Mr. O'Keefe, and Ms. Perez were, how much better Danielle looked than in the pictures we had seen, how energetic she was. Thankfully, before Dorothy could ask me any more questions, my cell phone rang. Saved by the bell.

I waved good-bye to Dorothy and answered the call. It was Bernie, wanting to know if I was still going through the files and if I had found out any more information. I told him I was on my way back to the house to do just that, so I could finish before Willie got home from school at three. Bernie normally got home from work around four, but he said he was going to skip lunch and come home early so we could talk.

Back at the kitchen table, I turned to the court testimony of Dr. Kathleen Armstrong, the psychologist Garet had taken Danielle to for testing. She worked at USF—the site of the stolen chicken leg incident. Dr. Armstrong had taken the stand as "an expert in child psychology." She stated that she had examined Danielle in October 2005 and described her as "pitiful."

Scanning ahead, I could see that "pitiful" was the good news. I rummaged around in the pencil holder by the phone to find a highlight marker. Bernie has a tendency to skim over things he doesn't want to see, and I wanted to be sure he got the whole picture, as bleak as it was.

> ... the child wandered around the room and had no communication skills with anyone in the room and could not use gestures or signs to express her thoughts or feelings. She made guttural sounds, had no "functional" play and failed to communicate with Dr. Armstrong or anyone else during the two hour period she was examined. . . . the child does not respond to her own name. . . . she does not engage with people. . . . she is small for her age. . . . walked on her tip toes (which is a form of neurological immaturity) and did not have much affect or emotional expression. . . . she "freaked out" if anyone tried to touch her. . . . The child wore a diaper (although she was seven years old) and could not feed herself. She feeds from a bottle but if finger fed, she choked.

Bernie and I had seen the odd tip-toe walk, as well as the constant motion. We knew about the diaper and that she had to be fed. We heard the guttural sounds, along with some bizarre animal-like screeching. But we also saw a difference in the year since Dr. Armstrong's examination and when we met her in Mr. O'Keefe's classroom. She had progressed from a bottle and was able to chew and swallow solid food as long as it was cut small. She didn't freak out when I started to change her diaper, at least not until I freaked out. She actually looked tall for her age to us. And she most definitely "engaged" with Bernie when she was on the swing.

That she had made so much progress in one year seemed promising to me. But as I read on, I felt like someone was turning off all of the lights in the room until all that was visible were the streaks of Day-Glo green highlight marker on the typewritten pages.

The child is severely to profoundly mentally retarded, scoring below the one (1) percentile. . . . the child's cognitive skills at the level of a two-month-old baby. . . . the child's motor skills at the level of a 27-month-old toddler. The child's global score was 50, showing that she was quite developmentally delayed. . . . the child is not autistic. . . . could find no physical basis for this child's condition. . . . found no medical reasons for this child's condition. . . . . the condition could be the result of severe neglect and deprivation. The information from the child's history was consistent with severe neglect. . . . Dr. Armstrong testified that eighty percent of development happens in the first five years of life. . . . The lack of early intervention or stimulation could have contributed to the child's permanent inability to communicate with others. She expects the child will not learn to talk and her prognosis is very poor. . . . If the child had received early intervention, in her opinion, she might have done better. . . . The child is now almost 8 years old. The lack of stimulation in her environment of the last 7 years contributed to her severe condition.

I felt as if I had been kicked in the gut, all of the air violently expelled from my body, then rage rising in me like bile.

"If the child had received early intervention, in her opinion, she might have done better."

That statement reminded me of something I had read in an article by Dr. Bruce Perry, a child psychiatrist and an expert on the effects of severe neglect on child development, and that I had bookmarked on the computer. There they were, three little words that stood out as if they were framed in blinking neon lights on a stadium Jumbotron. "Timing is everything."

In the article Dr. Perry wrote that "the time in life when the brain is most sensitive to experience—and therefore most easy to influence in positive and negative ways—is in infancy and early childhood. It is during these times in life when social, emotional, cognitive and physical experiences will shape neural systems in ways that influence functioning for a lifetime."

Side-by-side CT scans of the brains of two three-year-old children—one of a healthy child, and the other of a child who had suffered severe sensory-deprivation neglect—showed the neglected one to have a significantly smaller brain. Experience plays a crucial role in the "wiring" of a child's brain.

Areas of the brain develop, organize, and become fully functional during different times in childhood, and each area has its own timetable. There are "windows of opportunity" that must be taken advantage of or, ultimately, that window will close. Contrary to the cliché, in brain development when one door closes, it does not mean a window will open.

Early childhood is the most intensive period of brain development during the life span. The really crucial years for language development are from two to five years old, although the groundwork is laid even prior to that by exposure to language and by caregivers speaking to children.

In every aspect of child development, early nurturing is essential. Brain and biological development during the first years of life is highly influenced by an infant's environment. During early childhood (from the prenatal period to eight years of age), children must spend time in a caring, responsive environment that protects them from neglect and inappropriate disapproval and punishment.

Deprivation of key experiences during development may be the most destructive type of child maltreatment. The earlier and more pervasive the neglect is, the more devastating the developmental problems for the child, and the degree of recovery from severe neglect is inversely proportional to the age that the child was when removed from the neglecting caregivers.

Timing is everything. How much difference would it have made if Danielle had been removed from her mother's home the first time the DCF came to investigate a claim of abuse when she was not yet four years old? When every window had not yet closed? Instead, it took three more window-of-opportunity years for Danielle to finally be taken from Michelle Crockett's "adequate care."

I found myself thinking, "If only her mother had hit her or her brother bitten her." Abuse is easier to recognize than neglect is. At least, until neglect gets to the stage when it is absolutely undeniable, as it was when Detective Holste carried Danielle out of her house. By then, the damage was done. Timing is everything.

There was nothing Bernie or I could do about the past; it was done, as Bernie liked to remind me. But maybe timing could also work in Danielle's favor. Our timing. I had wanted to adopt forever, but the timing was never right. I had been a single mother for most of the time Paul and Steven were growing up. Then Bernie and I had five boys in the house, and we barely had room, money, or time for the children we had. The timing was wrong.

But as, one by one, they left the nest, the desire to adopt grew in me. During that period of time, Bernie went from being completely opposed to less resistant to vaguely interested to open to it to so onboard you would have thought that adopting was his idea all along.

Maybe timing was everything. And this time, it was finally going to be working for Danielle, rather than against her. Maybe her time was coming.

12

Step by Step

I looked at the clock in the kitchen and saw that there wasn't much time left before Willie would be home from school and Bernie from work, so I quickly read through the rest of the trial transcript, since I already knew the outcome.

I did study the mother's testimony, thinking she might offer some insight on Danielle that could be helpful, even if she hadn't intended it to be. I assumed she did what all witnesses are required to do—put her hand on the Bible and swore to tell the truth, the whole truth, and nothing but the truth. But in response to some questions, she either asserted her right to remain silent or she lied.

The mother claimed Danielle could say "mommy," "I love you," "eat," and "let's go," explaining that the reason no one else could hear her was because the child spoke so softly, and one had to really listen. The mother claimed to have taken Danielle to the park but couldn't name the park. She said Danielle had often slept with her, except when she had a boyfriend, and then Danielle was put on the mattress on the floor that was pushed up beside another mattress where her nineteen-year-old son slept. The mother claimed to have bathed Danielle daily and to have put her on the toilet fifteen to twenty times a day in an attempt to potty-train her.

Unfortunately for the mother, the document stated that the court did not find her to be a credible witness in the case and would not accept her testimony as true.

I skipped ahead to the final section, "Conclusions of Law," and it got straight to the point: "Based upon the foregoing, the Court finds that the Department has proven by clear and convincing evidence that the mother Michelle Crockett's parental rights should be terminated as to the child, Danielle Crockett." And so they were.

I was straightening up all of the papers when Bernie got home, eager to hear what I had found out. Since he already had a pretty good idea from the *Child Study* of the conditions Danielle had been living under and why she was removed from the home, I wanted to share with him what I had learned about neglect and child development and talk about what we might see down the road. Sure, the story about Danielle swiping the chicken leg right off the lady's plate at Dr. Armstrong's office was funny when Garet told it, but how funny would it be in a restaurant when some stranger was glaring at us because Danielle had his pork chop in her mouth?

Her constant movement was exhausting to watch, much less monitor. Willie has attention-deficit/hyperactivity disorder (ADHD), and when he gets really hyped up, it's hard to keep him focused and on task. What would happen with a little Tasmanian devil running around? How would Willie handle it? How would I handle it? He can get on my nerves when he's all over the place, touching everything, going on and on about something, anything. "I saw a dog today with five toes!" Three hours later, we're still talking about the five-toed dog.

I pointed out to Bernie that Willie can get on his nerves, too, even though Bernie isn't the one sitting on top of him to do his homework or nagging him to clean his room. I said, "Don't you think Danielle would get on your nerves?" He shook his head. No. Simple as that. No.

Bernie and I were not exactly on the same wavelength. He was thinking, "Oh, yeah, we'll take her." He wasn't really thinking it through or considering the possible ramifications.

I reminded him of Danielle's developmental markers in the *Child Study*, nearly all of which corresponded with those of a child under one year of age. Developmental pediatricians had concluded that her development from a physical level—gross and fine motor skills—as well as her speech and social abilities, were approximately those of a six-month-old.

Bernie wasn't budging. He, in turn, reminded me that those tests had been taken immediately or soon after she had been taken into state custody. He pointed out that in the car on the way home from Tampa, I had pooh-poohed those assessments. "We saw her," he said. "You are the one who said that she was already much further along after a year in school. You are the one who wondered if anyone had ever tried to toilet-train her or teach her to drink from a cup or feed herself or if everyone believed there was nothing that could be done."

Thinking about toilet training was one thing. Doing it was another, especially when the un-potty-trained child was an eight-year-old who couldn't sit still. I wondered if there was a window of opportunity for toilet training and self-feeding that we had missed as well.

I told him about the key times for child development being in infancy and early childhood. That what we learn in those years affects us for a lifetime. That those windows for learning have an expiration date. That in every aspect of child development that exists, early nurturing is crucial.

I pulled out the TPR trial papers and found Dr. Armstrong's testimony, all of the discouraging news highlighted in phosphorescent green. I pointed at the sentence "Eighty percent of development happens in the first 5 years of life. She expects the child will not learn to talk."

Bernie looked at me. "Well, the good news is she won't chatter us to death like Willie." I wasn't in the mood for joking. Or sarcasm. I couldn't tell which one he was resorting to.

He took the papers from me and skimmed over the highlighted parts, turning the pages quickly until he stopped on one, his fingers clenching the papers tightly. I looked over his shoulder at what he was reading. It was in the final section, "Conclusions of the Law." "Danielle is non-verbal and due to her profound disabilities, she appears to be unable to demonstrate love for another person. . . . Due to her profound disabilities, the Court is unable to determine whether Danielle is capable of forming any significant relationship with a parental substitute or any other person."

I knew exactly what Bernie was thinking, because it was what I was thinking. I thought back to the first day we saw her photo at GameWorks when the agency people told us we didn't want her and that was all it took to steer us onto this path. I remember telling Bernie that she needed us, and he agreed.

Now I was feeling more doubt than he was, but I was also trying to be more practical and realistic. He worked every day; I was the stay-at-home mom. Caring for Danielle would be a 24/7 responsibility, and much of that 24 and most of those 7s would be mine alone.

It was time to meet Willie at the bus stop, and Bernie came along. He took my hand, and we walked silently, both of us lost in our own thoughts. The same words that jumped out at him kept repeating themselves in my mind. "She appears to be unable to demonstrate love for another person."

How could she demonstrate love? She had never in her entire life been loved by a mother or a father, the very people who first show us what love is. She didn't have a single clue about what love was. Maybe if she was loved, unconditionally, fiercely loved, she would learn to love back.

When the bus pulled up, I saw Willie's face through the window, looking anxious at the unusual sight of his dad at the bus stop, too. He clambered down the stairs, asking, "What's wrong?" I told him nothing was wrong, that Dad had come home early so we could talk about Danielle. All the way home, Willie asked questions. "How old is she? Is she smaller than me? Is she nice? What is her school like? Where does she live?"

We answered him as best and honestly as we could. I told him that when we first talked about adopting, we had hoped to bring a child into our family whom he could play and hang out with. Who would be not only a sibling but a friend and a companion. I told him that the way Danielle was now, she would not be that playmate. She needed lots of care and patience and love, and it wouldn't be easy. Bernie told Willie that he was a big part of the decision because it was just the three of us in the house now, and his feelings were our priority.

Willie looked very thoughtful. He is a serious boy, sometimes too serious. He was so small for his age that he didn't roughhouse with the other boys in school, and he struggled with assignments because of his ADHD. On the other hand, he could sit for hours making miniature furniture, a hobby he had picked up a couple of years earlier.

Willie's heart was the heart of a giant. He had always been that way—compassionate, caring, and empathetic. He loved animals as much as I did and was always kind and helpful to the younger children at church. He was also a little boy, barely nine years old, and I don't know many children who don't think the world revolves around them.

He looked from me to Bernie and back to me again, his eyes wide, and asked, "Do I have to make up my mind right now? Can

I meet her?" I answered, "No!" at the same time that Bernie said, "Yes!" Poor Willie, he looked so confused. I told him that what we meant was, no, he did not have to make up his mind right then, and yes, he could meet her.

Bernie and I looked at the clock at the same time. It was 4:25—twenty-four hours and twenty minutes since we had signed the *Study of the Child* papers. Twenty minutes past the minimal amount of time we could take to decide whether we wanted a second visit with Danielle.

Bernie pulled Garet's card out of his pocket and dialed the number, putting it on speaker phone. She must have been waiting for us, because she answered immediately. "This is Garet White." "Garet, this is Bernie Lierow. Diane and I would like a second visit with Danielle, and we would like to bring our son William along. We hope that's okay."

I could hear Garet's smile through the phone line. "Okay?! That's fantastic. How's next Monday?" "Perfect!" I practically shouted. "We'll see you at the school Monday!"

13

Meet the Family

Paul came to visit us over the weekend, picking up some things he hadn't moved to his apartment yet. He and Steven had expressed support to us, as well as to the interviewer for the Home Study of our desire to adopt. But that was when they thought we'd be bringing home a "normal" little boy or girl. Someone who talked, walked, and could go boogie boarding with them or to see the kids' movies they were embarrassed to admit they still liked.

But they were both skeptical of bringing someone like Danielle into the family and into our home. Skeptical might be understating Paul's reaction the night we all watched *Nell*. "Are you two insane? Have you lost your minds?" Paul has always had a dramatic way of expressing himself. Besides, I think these were rhetorical questions because he had already decided we had lost our minds.

Steven didn't say much, but that was his way. I could tell he was thinking it was not a good idea. He spent most of his time with his girlfriend or at work, so maybe he felt as if he didn't have a vote.

I told Paul that we were going to see Danielle for a second visit on Monday and were taking Willie with us. He surprised me by asking if he could come along, too. Bernie called Garet to check that it was okay to bring another member of the family, and she actually seemed pleased.

That Monday morning we drove up to Tampa. I tried to tell Paul and Willie what to expect, not just from Danielle, but from the other children in Mr. O'Keefe's room. I explained to them what *profound needs* meant: that the children couldn't speak and would probably not even acknowledge our presence, and that most of the kids in that room were in wheelchairs, in large cribs, or on mats.

The closer we got, the quieter Willie became. I asked him if something was wrong or bothering him, and in a quavering voice he confessed, "I'm scared and nervous. What if she doesn't like me? What if she starts screaming at me? What if she acts so weird I can't take it?" Paul looked up from his book and told Willie he was scared, too, and gave Willie a reassuring squeeze around his shoulders. I made a mental note to bake him a batch of brownies when we got back home.

The four of us crowded into the tiny reception area of the school where Garet was already talking to Principal Middleton. She was glad to see us and very welcoming to Willie and Paul. Ms. Perez came out of her office and told us she was going that way and would take us there.

Walking across the campus on sidewalks that connected the buildings to each other, we ran into a pair of students who looked like they were about Willie's age. They stopped to say hello to Ms. Perez, and she introduced us to them. "Boys, this is Mr. and Mrs. Lierow, Paul, and William." One of them asked Willie if he was coming to the school, and he shook his head no. Ms Perez said, "We are going to Mr. O'Keefe's room to see Danielle." The boys smiled. "Are you her family?" one asked eagerly. Awkward pause.

"No," Bernie said. "We're just friends, and we've come to visit with her for the day." That satisfied them, and we continued, with Willie looking back over his shoulder as if he wished he was going in their direction and not ours.

Ms. Perez asked us to wait in the hall while she went in to make sure Mr. O'Keefe wasn't in the middle of something or there wasn't a crisis in the classroom. Peeking through the window, I could see Danielle wandering about the room and remarked that the T-shirt she was wearing looked awfully small. Garet leaned over my shoulder to look in the window. "No wonder," she said. "That's one of the shirts I bought her when she got out of the hospital. She didn't have any clothes. She's grown quite a bit in a year."

Ms. Perez opened the door, and we filed in—me, Bernie, Paul, William, and Garet bringing up the rear. We waved to Mr. O'Keefe, who was engaged with one of his students. Paul's eyes were scanning the room, his expression somewhere between shock and curiosity. Willie simply stood wide-eyed. Bernie, Garet, and I all said, "Hi, Danielle!" in our brightest, cheeriest voices at the same time, which stopped her in her tracks, although she didn't look at us. She dropped the ball she was holding on the floor, circled the table on her tippy toes in that odd way she had, and then she saw Willie. As if on a mission, she walked directly to him, grabbed hold of each forearm, and stared into his eyes for a good thirty seconds. Willie was frozen like a statue, holding her stare. Then, as abruptly as she had approached him, she let his arms go and ran off. We were all dumbfounded, except Mr. O'Keefe, who was smiling at Willie. "I think you've made a friend," he said quietly.

It definitely broke the tension. Bernie had brought a pink plastic Slinky with him and went to see if he could use that to entice Danielle to play again. Sure enough, she followed him over to the swing, and he pulled her back and forth with the Slinky. Did she remember doing that with him on our first visit, did she connect him with the swing and the Slinky, or were swings and Slinkys that irresistible to her?

Willie and I sat with Garet watching them—especially Willie, who was just taking it all in. When he saw one of the mobile students struggling with a toy, he went over to help, and they played together. Paul pushed the kids in wheelchairs around the classroom and helped take them outside when it was time for recess.

Mr. O'Keefe asked me if I wanted to change Danielle before lunch, and I was grateful that he gave me another chance. This time, it went off without a hitch, but it was still disconcerting. What would it be like when she hit puberty if she was still in a diaper? Would she move into Depends when she was fully grown?

At lunch, we surrounded her, Willie on one side of her, Paul on the other, and Bernie and I across the table so we could take turns feeding her. After each bite, she would go around the circle of us, patting each of our hands while she chewed. Another bite, another round of pats. Willie, Paul, and Bernie were giggling like little girls. I was afraid of breaking whatever spell we were under, so I kept feeding her but slowed it down to make the magic happening right then at that table last as long as possible. As soon as the food was gone, she jumped up and bolted away. We all looked at one another in disbelief, as if we had just been released from a spell. At the table next to us, Mr. O'Keefe was fairly beaming.

Bernie, despite the magic, wanted to beat the school buses out of Tampa and the rush hour back home. Although the bridge onto Estero Island is four lanes, it funnels onto the two-lane road that runs from the north end to the south end, and from four to six every weekday evening, it is a linear parking lot.

Garet didn't even need to ask us this time if we wanted to come back for a third visit, although we had to follow procedure and wait twenty-four hours to call and schedule it. We gathered up our things and said good-bye to Mr. O'Keefe. Willie went to find the two students he had been playing with, and Paul made the rounds of the classroom aides. Danielle was wandering around the room again. We kept saying, "Bye, Danielle, bye-bye, Danielle," but she ignored us. As Garet opened the door for us to go, Danielle ran over to us, just as she had with Willie in the morning, but this time Paul was the target. She wrapped her arms around him in a big bear hug, looked up at him, and then ran off. The look on his face was priceless, and we all laughed.

But in the car, Paul broke down. He had never seen children as disabled as the ones in Mr. O'Keefe's classroom, with so many needs. He put his head in his hands and sobbed. I felt helpless, and I reached to the backseat and patted one of Paul's knees while Willie patted the other. Bernie kept his eyes on the road, occasionally glancing at Paul in the rearview mirror. When Paul pulled himself together, he lifted his head up, his eyes red, face wet from tears, and said, "I didn't know! Compared to the ones who can't walk or move any part of their body, Danielle is so lucky."

Out of the mouths of babes, or twenty-one-year-olds. We were all quiet, thinking of what Paul said. Looking at it that way, he was absolutely right. Danielle was lucky.

That night, Bernie and I lay in bed talking about the way Danielle had reacted to Willie and Paul and had patted our hands, one by one, at lunch. Mr. O'Keefe said he had never seen her do anything like that before. What did it mean? I told Bernie maybe God had been watching over her all along. He had shown her in some way that there was a family, and "they're going to come and get you and take care of you, and your life will be really different. Just hang on." That's how, against all odds, Danielle stayed alive. She knew we were coming before we came, and when we did come, she already knew us. Because that was how she reacted when we met, as if she already knew us. Was it that different from my reaction to seeing her photo for the first time, knowing nothing about her except that she needed us? Not some random family, but us, the Lierows—Bernie, Willie, and me.

When the alarm went off at five-thirty the next morning, Bernie was already awake and sitting up in bed. I asked him if something was wrong, and he shook his head. "I had the strangest dream, you know, one of those dreams so real that when you wake up, you're not sure if it was a dream? I don't even know where I was, but first I saw Danielle, she was sitting on something. I thought maybe it was a big swing, since she likes to swing so much. Then it was like a movie camera pulling back and the picture got bigger, and I realized she was sitting in a giant pair of hands, cupped hands. Everything around the hands was dark, but the hands were coming forward, holding Danielle. She looked like Tinkerbell perched on those hands. Then I heard a voice, and it said, 'She was mine, and now she's yours. Take care of her.' The hands set her gently down and pulled away. That was it."

I had chill bumps. God speaks to us in many ways—through prayer, nature, children, in acts of kindness and sacrifice. I'm sure God speaks to us far more than we know and far more than we notice in the hustle bustle of our lives. God chose a time to speak to Bernie when everything was quiet and Bernie would hear. It was a powerful message and one we knew we couldn't ignore, even if we wanted to at that point.

When Bernie got home from work, he called Garet and we made arrangements for the third visit. HKI policy says there have to be three meetings between the child and the adoptive parents before the child can make a visit to the home. We could have met Danielle at locations other than the school, but the only places she ever went were school and the foster home, and the foster parents did not want us to come there. That made me curious—was there something they were hiding from us, or did they just want to protect their privacy? So, a few days later, Bernie and I drove back to Tampa again to Sanders Memorial for our third meeting.

Danielle seemed to know us this time. She had taken to Bernie very quickly. Everyone who saw them remarked about it. She was slower to come to me. Garet theorized that she might have a problem with "mothers," per se, after the way she had been treated by her own mother. We had no way of knowing whether during the seven years Danielle lived with her, Michelle Crockett had ever hit her, screamed at her, or threatened her in some way. I didn't want to push it. I wanted Danielle to feel safe and come to me when she was ready. Still, I have to admit I was a little envious of the comfort level she had with Bernie.

While Bernie was playing with Danielle, Garet and I talked about how the home visit would work. It would be for a weekend, hopefully within the next couple of weeks. Garet would talk to the foster parents to make sure there was no conflict. We would come to the school to pick her up on a Friday afternoon, then bring her back on Sunday to the foster home.

When it was time to go, Bernie gave her a big hug. I squatted in front of her so she could see my face and told her that the next time we saw her, she would be coming home with us. That we would swim in our pool, go to the beach, and play with Willie and our dogs. I don't know if she had any idea what I was talking about, but she followed Bernie and me to the door, and when we opened it to leave, she tried to come with us. Mr. O'Keefe had to come over and hold onto her so we could get out.

Bernie was so upset, he didn't want to go at all. I was, too, but I reminded him of the evaluation in the TPR papers that concluded it couldn't be determined whether Danielle was capable of forming any significant relationship with a parental substitute or any other person. That Danielle tried to come with us showed me that she was already forming a relationship with us. How significant it was, I couldn't say, but it was a start. That cheered Bernie up a bit.

On the way home, we talked about where Danielle would sleep in the house. In our house, almost everything was on the second level—the living room, the kitchen and the dining room, the master bedroom and bath, a second bedroom and bath, and a huge deck off the back. The first floor had the largest bedroom and bathroom and had been Steven and Paul's room when we first got the house. The laundry room was down there, along with an area between those rooms and the sliding doors to the outside that we didn't use as a room, but it had furniture in it. The screened pool and the hot tub were outside the sliding glass doors. Beyond the screened enclosure was the backyard, and beyond that, our small dock.

Bernie and I had the master bedroom, and Willie had the other bedroom upstairs. Obviously, with as much supervision as Danielle needed—we had been told she did not sleep through the night—she could not be downstairs by herself. We couldn't move downstairs and leave the two kids upstairs by themselves. I wasn't sure how Willie would feel about moving downstairs.

We sat down with him and explained the situation. He was anxious, but he knew it was the only way it could work. It was Willie who came up with the idea of walkie-talkies, and I told him if it would make him feel better, I could dig out the baby monitors I had used for him and his older brothers.

I was so grateful to him for being so sweet about it. Bernie said he would paint the room whatever color Willie wanted, and I tried to convince Willie how much fun it would be to redecorate. The next morning, we went to Lowe's first to buy paint and then to Wal-Mart for the walkie-talkies and the new sheets and spreads for the twin beds in that room. I thought I could shop for things for Danielle's room while Willie was at school.

On our way to the checkout line, we passed a big display for Valentine candy, and I told Bernie to go on ahead with Willie so that I could pick up some things for him and Danielle. This would be her first Valentine's Day holiday, and I wanted it to be memorable.

At home, Bernie and Willie got to work painting the downstairs bedroom. I sat on the floor in Willie's bedroom and thought, "If I were an eight-year-old girl, what would I want my room to look like?" I had hands-on experience only with boys, and I didn't know any eight-year-old girls, other than the ones in Willie's class at school and church. They were either whispering secrets or squealing at an ear-shattering pitch, and they all smelled fruity-sweet. They looked very high maintenance and a little bit scary to me.

Bernie came into the room with his phone up to his ear and an anxious look on his face. I could hear only one side of the conversation. "Why?" "Can they do that?" "Why are they waiting until now?" "What can we do?" "When will we find out?" "I understand." "No, we know you're doing everything you can." "All right, thanks. Call us when you know something. Bye, Garet."

Garet? That wasn't good. I thought he had been talking to a contractor about a job. If it was Garet, it had to be about Danielle. Bernie was clearly upset, not mad-upset but sad-upset. "Garet said there were some problems, and it might take longer than we wanted for Danielle to come for a visit." Trying not to shoot the messenger, I asked as calmly as I could what kind of problems.

Immediately after Michelle Crockett's parental rights had been terminated in September 2006, she was appointed an appellate counsel for the purpose of filing an appeal. Nothing happened for a long while, but right around the time we made our first visit to the school to meet Danielle, the appellant requested and received an extension of time for sixty days.

Although it didn't make sense to us—little about this case made sense to us—it had been suggested that visits be put on hold until more was known about the appeal. I couldn't believe that Michelle Crockett was given the right to appeal, and I didn't understand why she wanted to. She had treated Danielle worse than a yard dog when she had the child. Why would she want Danielle back?

On top of that, the foster mother where Danielle was currently living was not being very cooperative in making arrangements for a weekend visit.

The bottom line was, Garet would keep pushing for it, but she couldn't say when we might get to have Danielle for an in-home visit. Garet had assured Bernie that she knew in her heart that Danielle belonged with us, that we were meant to have Danielle, and that she would do everything in her power to make it happen. Unfortunately, she could not assure us that this was just a legal technicality and would definitely be resolved in Danielle's favor.

But we knew how much Garet loved Danielle and that this case was personal for her. Garet had told us that right from the start, even before we came into the picture, she'd had a good feeling that Danielle would find a family. When we were so persistent that day at GameWorks, Garet had wondered whether we were that family. When she saw how Danielle reacted to Bernie in the classroom, she knew that we were. She believed this was meant to be, that we were the ones.

I told Bernie that everything that had happened so far had led us to Danielle, and surely the next step would be to bring her home. It might take longer than we would like, we may have to overcome obstacles, but I didn't believe that God would knock on our door and lead us down this path if we weren't meant to be together. We could not get discouraged, and we had to have faith.

Monday morning, after Bernie went to work and Willie got on the school bus, I drove straight to Wal-Mart. For the first time in my mothering career, I steered my cart to the girls' department—an alien world of pink, glitter, hair ribbons, and sweet, fruity smells.

14

Hello Kitty

When Bernie wants something, he will be your worst nightmare until he gets it. Poor Garet, I'm surprised she didn't have his number blocked on her phone. He must have called a couple of times a week to see if there was any progress toward the home visit, but her hands were tied and she felt as helpless as we did.

Dealing with the DCF was like driving your car into a brick wall, backing up, and driving into it again, over and over. It's no wonder there are so many children waiting to be adopted and so many children who eventually age out of the foster-care system without ever finding a family. We appreciate the DCF's diligence in making sure that children are placed in safe and loving homes and that the best matches are made, but we also understand why good and qualified people eventually give up.

We were frustrated, Garet was frustrated, and in the middle was a little girl lost in limbo. We had told her on our last visit that the next time we saw her, we would be taking her home with us to visit, and then we didn't even show up for a couple of months.

I have read that dogs have no concept of time—that their people can be gone for ten minutes or ten days or ten weeks and it is all the same to them. Danielle probably didn't know the difference between ten days and ten weeks. She just knew that the people who told her they would come back and take her to the beach had not kept their word. It was heartbreaking that we couldn't even send her a message.

One thing we were required to do as part of the adoption process was make a scrapbook of photos of our family, home, animals, and interests to give to the social worker to show to the child prior to the first meeting. It was intended to introduce the child to the family before an actual face-to-face meeting. I made a scrapbook that showed several views of our house, front and back; a very handsome picture of Willie and Bernie wearing matching dress shirts on their way to church one morning; the big dog Spice and me in our backyard; the pool and the hot tub; two of our three little dogs on the stairs to the deck; the dock and the canal; our church; Willie's school; and Willie playing on the beach.

Standard operating procedure was always a little different with Danielle, and there was no point in showing her the scrapbook before she met us. She would not have understood what she was seeing. But we brought the album with us on our first visit and left it with Garet. Maybe she had been showing it to Danielle while we were separated from her. Or maybe, given all of the brick walls we encountered during the last couple of months, Garet thought it best not to get Danielle's hopes up.

In our eternal optimism—or stupendous naivety—we had proceeded with the plan to flip bedrooms. We didn't want to allow the possibility to come into our heads that the adoption would never happen. We knew the call telling us that a visit had been approved could come out of the blue, and that is exactly what happened.

Garet called Bernie the last week of March and told him that Danielle would have a week off the next week for spring break and that Garet was allowed to send her home with us for three days. Could we do that? Bernie was at work and told me later that he was afraid that if he asked for five minutes to get me on the phone to discuss it, they would change their minds, so he just blurted out, "Yes!" Then he waited until he got home to tell me, because he said he wanted to see my face when I got the news. It was his face—with a grin from ear to ear—that gave it away the second he walked in the door. "Did Garet call?" "Yes!" "When do we get her?" "Friday!" "Friday? Friday two days from now Friday or Friday next week Friday?" "Friday two days from now!"

It was Wednesday evening, which gave me one day to shop for groceries and a big supply of pull-up diapers.

Danielle's room had been ready for weeks. Bernie, Willie, and I decorated it together, our idea of what a little girl's room should look like, which was a lot of pink. I bought a bright pink Hello Kitty comforter, Hello Kitty pillows, and Hello Kitty sheets for the trundle bed she was inheriting from Willie. Hello Kitty looked so happy that I couldn't help but smile every time I saw that funny little face. I put framed prints on the wall and a couple of small rugs on the ceramic tile floor. There were two windows—one looked out to the street in front of the house and framed the top of a palm tree; the other had a bird's eye view of Bill and Doris's house and pool on the corner. Currently, there was a six-foot-tall inflated pink Easter bunny holding a giant Easter egg in their front yard. I was a little worried that it might scare Danielle, so I told myself I needed to remember to keep that shade drawn. We didn't know yet what her sleeping habits were, so I also hung some curtains to block more of the bright Florida sun.

We moved a large white cupboard from downstairs up to her room and put the (pink) dress, (pink) sandals, and (pink) hair bows I had gotten for her inside. Willie helped pile the top shelf of a small white wooden bookcase unit with at least two dozen stuffed animals—some from his own collection and others he picked out every time we were in a store. He put the bigger ones on the bed against the Hello Kitty pillows. On the bottom shelf we put children's picture books, old favorites that Willie had long ago outgrown. "Mom, remember *Brown Bear, Brown Bear*? And *Goodnight Moon*? I can read them to Danielle when she comes!"

Bernie added the finishing touch—a jumbo-size pink plastic Slinky on her white nightstand. I found myself walking past the room a dozen times a day just to look at it, I was so excited for her to see it.

We decided to take Willie out of school that day so he could go with us to Land O' Lakes to pick Danielle up. It was nearly a three-hour drive from the school to our house, and she would need some company in the backseat. I sent a note with Willie to the teacher, letting her know he would not be in school the next day.

I asked Bernie for Garet's number so I could see if there was anything we should do to prepare the house, other than what we had already done. Garet told me she had already spoken to Principal Middleton and Mr. O'Keefe, and they were so glad that the visit was finally taking place. Garet had also spoken to the foster mother to see if she had any suggestions for us in making Danielle as comfortable as possible in our home. Obviously, Danielle had never been on a sleepover before.

What Garet said dumbfounded me. The foster mother recommended that we strip the bedroom where Danielle would be sleeping of everything but the mattress—which should be on the floor—and the bedding. The foster mother said that if there was any other furniture, Danielle would climb on it; that if there were curtains on the windows, she would tear them down; and if there were pictures on the wall, she would pull them off.

I was speechless, mad, and sad at the same time. Finally, Garet said, "Diane, are you there?" I asked her how this was any better than Michelle Crockett's home. Garet pointed out that this house was clean; that Danielle's room wasn't full of trash, bugs, and animal feces; and that she was in school and she was cared for. She wasn't cared for in the same way we wanted to care for her, but she was not an easy child to place. She was not handicapped in a way that would put her in a medical foster home, but she had so many needs that she couldn't be placed in a "regular" foster home. The only alternative would have been an institution.

I knew Garet was getting Danielle the best possible care she could, and I didn't want to seem ungrateful, so I thanked her again for pushing so hard to make this happen and told her we'd see her at the school tomorrow afternoon.

When Bernie came home from work, Willie was doing his homework in the kitchen, and I was sitting on Danielle's bed with Cece, Bebe, and Inky in my lap, trying not to cry. I told him what the foster home had told Garet about the bedroom and saw a flash of anger cross his face, too. "That's ridiculous. You made this room for her, and we're keeping it exactly the way it is. If she takes pictures off the wall or tears the curtains down, we'll deal with it then. What's for dinner?"

Before we left the next morning, Willie put some of the stuffed animals and the toys we had gotten Danielle in the backseat. I had a bag packed with pull-up diapers, baby wipes, towels, and Goldfish crackers and a cooler with juice boxes and grapes. I felt like I was packing for a toddler and not an eight-year-old.

Once again, we met Garet in the main office and then went to Mr. O'Keefe's room to get Danielle. We were all nervous about how she would react. Would she remember us? We walked into the classroom, and although she didn't run across the room to greet us, she made brief eye contact and gave Willie a little smile. I walked over to her and asked if she wanted me to rock her. We got in the rocker together, and for the first time since we'd met, I was holding her as I would my own baby girl. I whispered, "Rock, rock, rock,

Danielle," in her ear, and very quietly she repeated, "Rah," to me. Or maybe it was what I wanted to hear so badly that I did.

We got instructions from Garet on Danielle's medication and some insight into her sleeping habits. We knew she was on medication—her tongue kind of hung out the side of her mouth, and she drooled, so much so that the front of her shirt was always wet. I assumed that this was from the drugs. She was on antipsychotic medication and was getting the maximum adult dosage twice a day. I wondered whether it was because she was even more hyper when she was not on drugs, or if the drugs just made caring for her easier for the foster parents. Mr. O'Keefe told us the medication made Danielle very dry-mouthed and thirsty, so she drank lots of water. Which meant she went through lots of diapers.

Garet told us the foster mother said that Danielle had terrible sleep patterns, that she slept only a couple of hours at a time at most and she became violent. Violent with whom or what? She was by herself in a stripped-down room with nothing but a mattress and sheets. We also learned that her bedroom door—kept closed when she was in there—was equipped with an alarm so that the foster parents would know if she got up to wander through the house in the middle of the night.

Garet handed us Danielle's backpack, which the foster mother had packed with clothes. I put a fresh diaper on her, and we were ready to go. Mr. O'Keefe, Ms. Perez, and Garet were lined up in the hall, looking like parents watching their child go off to college. Smiling, waving, they tried to look brave as their eyes filled with tears. "'Bye, Danielle, have fun! Happy Easter!" Danielle looked back briefly, then came willingly with us to the main office to sign her out and to the car, where Willie and the stuffed animals lured her into the backseat. Bernie buckled her up, and we were off. I felt as free and giddy as a teenager on a road trip with Daddy's car and credit card.

We had no idea how Danielle would do on a long ride. Willie was a good car rider, content to read books, fiddle with his Etch-a-Sketch or work puzzles. We didn't have a DVD player for movies in the car. I believe children need breaks from screen time, and there was plenty to see out the window. If Willie ever got really bored, I got out one of the car games books we always traveled with and opened it to a random page, and we all played together.

Danielle had gathered several of the stuffed animals into her arms and seemed happy looking out the window. I could see Bernie watching her and Willie in the rearview mirror, and I poked him in the side. "Keep your eyes on the road, Bernie!" He smiled. I smiled. It was the perfect Florida spring day, Easter was coming, and I felt as if we were part of a heaven-sent rebirth. We were so happy to have Danielle with us, just the four of us, away from everyone else.

Garet had told us Danielle loved McDonald's French fries, so we pulled off the interstate in Venice, which is about midway home. Helping Danielle out of the backseat, I saw that she had peed right through her diaper, her jeans, the towel I had put down, and the seat itself. Willie looked embarrassed, Bernie baffled, Danielle clueless, and I was perplexed. Should I change her in the car? It was awfully public in that busy parking lot. On the other hand, it didn't seem right to walk her though McDonald's with soaking-wet pants. I asked Bernie to get me some shorts from her bag of clothes in the trunk. He handed me a pair that was obviously too big, which I pointed out to him impatiently. He showed me the bag. "There's not much there, and all of what's there is the same." I pulled out some more shorts and a couple of tops. Everything was big, pulled in with safety pins. I guessed that they were hand-me-downs—maybe from another child who had lived in the house, but certainly not bought to fit Danielle. I was irritated, not just by the scant amount of clothes, but by the safety pins. Danielle wouldn't even be able to tell anyone if they came apart and were sticking her. I took the shorts that looked closest to her size, tied a sweatshirt of mine around her waist, grabbed the bag of pull-ups and wipes, and we walked into McDonald's, Bernie and William to order, Danielle and I to the rest room to change my sixty-pound baby.

Bernie chose a table inside toward the back, where he and Willie spread out the burgers and the fries. Danielle hadn't even sat down when she started shoving fries into her mouth until she couldn't chew, swallow, or close her mouth because the ends of fries were sticking out. Garet was right. Danielle sure loved her French fries. The three of us couldn't help but laugh, although the people staring at us from the surrounding tables didn't seem to get the joke. Bernie pulled fries gently out of her mouth until she had an amount she could chew and swallow, then handed the rest of them to her one at a time. She was ignoring her burger, so Willie pushed it close to her hands, picked his up, said, "Look, Danielle, this is how you do it," and took a bite. "Mmmm. It's really good." He got up to get ketchup for his fries, a tactical mistake.

As the woman in Dr. Armstrong's office at USF learned, never leave food unattended around Danielle. As soon as Willie turned his back, her little hand darted across the table and snatched a handful of fries. Aside from the fact that there were two witnesses to the theft, the evidence was still sticking out of her mouth when Willie got back with the ketchup for his now depleted pile of fries. His mouth and eyes widened at the same time. Bernie and I were laughing again, at Danielle and at the expression on poor Willie's face. Once again, Bernie pulled the fries out of her mouth, and I broke the burger into bite-size pieces to hand to her. Bite-size, yes; mess-free, no. By the time the burger was gone, Danielle was wearing as much of it as she had eaten, so it was back to the rest-room to wash her hands and face.

Except for stopping two more times to take Danielle to the bath-room and check her diaper—dry the first time, soaked the second—the rest of the trip was uneventful. We played children's music on the CD player, she looked out the window, rocked herself from side to side, "played" with her toys in the backseat, and made lots of strange noises. Kind of a humming-moaning-groaning-growling sound that was a low-pitched monotone. And then another that was more like a high-pitched "Woowoowoowoo." Bernie thought it sounded like a European ambulance. Was this her way of talking? Was she self-comforting in some way? After all, she was in an alien environment, going to an unknown destination with people she barely knew.

Steven was working at the north end of the island at one of the vacation properties, setting up umbrellas and renting out Jet Skis. We decided to stop there so that he and Danielle could meet and we could take her onto the beach for her first time.

Their meeting was a bit awkward. Steven was busy, and Danielle was bouncing up to her tip-toes and down on her heels, making that funny moaning sound. Steven seemed at a loss for what to do—hugging didn't seem appropriate, and shaking hands was not an option. He reached out his hand rather clumsily but sweetly to pat her on the top of her head. She threw both arms up to cover her head, shrieked, and twisted away. Steven jumped back away from her at the same time that Bernie reached to comfort her. Clearly, Danielle did not like anyone approaching her head. Was this another souvenir Michelle Crockett had left Danielle with?

Steven looked happy for the opening to get back to work, and we turned toward the beach. The gulf was about two hundred feet across the sand, and knowing this was Danielle's first time, we walked and talked all the way to the water. "Danielle, this is the beach. We are walking on sand. Those are seagulls. These are shells. Can you pick one up? That is the ocean. Those are waves. Do you want to go in the water? Let's take off our shoes." Shriek! Danielle did not like the sand on her bare feet one bit and nearly jumped into Bernie's arms. The sand was barely lukewarm at that time of year, so I wondered what had caused her extreme reaction.

Bernie walked her into the water and set her down at about knee depth, and she was fine. More than fine. She lifted her arms over her head and turned to the sun. A slight ocean breeze ruffled her hair. She closed her eyes, and a look of complete bliss covered her face. She bounced up and down. She giggled when the waves splashed onto her chest. She sat down and rolled in the waves, taking immediately and naturally to the water, like a little mermaid. Willie sat down beside her and splashed around with her, while Bernie and I smiled through our tears. I couldn't help but think this wasn't only her first time at the beach; it was her first time to be truly, purely happy. Over such a simple thing.

I hated to pull her out of the water, but I told her we needed to go see our dogs, and she allowed Bernie to carry her across the sand to the car. He guessed that her diaper probably weighed as much as she did. I wrapped her in a towel and buckled her into the backseat.

Dorothy and Paul's house was on the way to ours, so we pulled into their driveway and honked the horn. They came running out, smiling, eager to meet Danielle, but as Dorothy got closer to the car, her expression changed from excitement to apprehension. As she peered into the backseat, she blurted, "She looks like a poor little drowned rat!" I looked back at Danielle, and Dorothy was right. Danielle's hair was plastered to her head, her skin was still so pale, her eyes were red from the saltwater and she was shivering in the towel. I told them we'd see them after dinner during the evening dog walk.

At home, William and Bernie helped Danielle up the exterior stairs to the deck on the second floor, one of them beside her and one behind her. She wasn't used to long staircases. The dogs barked at her a couple of times, but she ignored them, and after sniffing her out, they ignored her, too. Inside, I took her to the bathroom right away to get her wet clothes off, towel her down, and put on a new pull-up diaper and another set of over-size dry clothes from her bag. I felt like I was really getting the hang of this.

We let her wander around the upstairs in the kitchen and the living room, getting acclimated to the family area. Willie was so excited for Danielle to see her room, he could barely contain himself. "Danielle, don't you want to see your bedroom? Come on," and he took her by the hand and led her down the hall, with Bernie and me behind them. The four of us then walked into Hello Kitty's Pink Palace.

Danielle's face lit up. She walked over to her bed and sat cross-legged among all of the pillows and the animals, beaming with joy. I have never seen anyone look as happy as she did at that moment. I was so glad we had not stripped the room, as the foster mother had advised. Every little girl deserves a pink room sometime in her life. This was Danielle's time.

We had dinner on the deck, all finger foods to make it easier for Danielle to feed herself: cut-up ham, raspberries, strawberries,

Diane with Danielle in her new bedroom.

In the bedroom on tippy toes, which is
how Danielle walked when the Lierows
first met her.

blackberries, blueberries, cheese and crackers, watermelon, and
chocolate milk. She felt everything before she put it in her mouth,
and she ate it all except the raspberries, which she spit out—
probably a texture thing. Blueberries were her favorite. I put milk
in her sippy cup and told her it needed to stay on the table, not on
the floor. I tapped the table for emphasis. She looked at me and
seemed to understand. The cup stayed on the table.

After dinner, we all went out with the dogs for the evening
walk. The morning wake-up walk was always brisk, with everyone
eager to let the dogs do their business, get back home, and get
the day started. But the postdinner neighborhood constitutional
was a social occasion, on some nights taking as long as two hours

for people to stop and chat, pick up a half pie, leftover grilled chicken, or a basket of garden tomatoes, comment on some new landscaping or outdoor lighting, or ask about the family.

Willie had one dog, I had the other two, and Bernie had Danielle as we started the circuitous route that took us through all of Laguna Shores. We ran into Dorothy right away, who apologized for calling Danielle a drowned rat. We just laughed. That was Dorothy's way. It didn't hurt our feelings, and we don't think it hurt Danielle's. We decided to take the shorter loop, thinking that everything might be too much for Danielle, being fawned over by so many strangers. Thanks to the close-knit nature of the neighborhood, everyone already knew who she was and was eager to welcome her and make a good impression.

Danielle wasn't responding very much to the notion of making new friends until we got to Doris and Bill's front yard and the giant pink Easter bunny with its enormous multicolored egg. Danielle pulled her hand out of Bernie's, loped over to the egg, and tried to climb up its surface. The thick plastic shell didn't offer a foothold of any kind, so each time she tried, she slipped back to the ground. But that didn't stop her from trying again. I loved the determination she was showing and added that to my mental list of her hidden qualities. Finally, Bernie couldn't stand it anymore, and he picked her up off the ground and brought her close to the bunny's face. Recognizing an opportunity when it was presented to her, she leaned toward the bunny, and, like a baby just learning to kiss, she opened her mouth wide and planted it on the bunny's fat pink cheek. The small crowd of neighbors who had gathered cheered her slobbery smacker. Not a bad debut for Danielle on her first night in Laguna Shores.

That warm, fuzzy feeling was short-lived. No sooner had we gotten into the house than Willie shouted, "Mom!" Bernie shouted, "Diane!" and both were looking at Danielle in horror as across the living room floor she trailed a stream of runny poop from her

The giant Easter Bunny in the neighbors' yard.

pants like lava running down the side of a volcano. I grabbed her up before she could reach the bedroom and carried her into the bathroom. I had dealt with diarrhea many times with my children, but Danielle was as oblivious to it as one of my baby goats back in Tennessee. She seemed a little scared when I put her in the walk-in shower stall, but I went ahead and got in with her, yelling to Bernie to bring me more towels, a pull-up diaper, and a change of clothes for her. He came in with a pair of shorts and a shirt, the next-to-last clean outfit that she had come with. I got her undressed, cleaned, dried, and redressed and sent her out of the bathroom with Bernie and a bottle of Kaopectate so that I could clean myself up.

Ten minutes later, another eruption and another trip to the shower for both of us. Bernie brought in the last of her clean clothes. I wondered what Danielle might have eaten, and Bernie sheepishly admitted that while they were playing in the water at the beach, he thought she had swallowed quite a bit. I rolled my eyes at him. We had learned through experience with Willie as a toddler that saltwater is quite a laxative.

It didn't seem like she could have much more in her, but I was wrong. Hoping that the third time was the charm, I finally put her in her pajamas, which was all that was left in the backpack anyway.

Not knowing how long it would take Danielle to fall asleep, I thought we should start early, so I gave her the bedtime medication dose they had sent, along with a couple of pieces of cheese as a supplement to the Kaopectate. Willie was watching television, so I told him to tell Danielle goodnight. He gave her a quick little hug, which she stood still for. Then she and I went back to the bedroom. Bernie came and tucked her in and left to sit with Willie before putting him to bed. Twice while I was reading her stories and playing songs from her musical Hello Kitty pillow, she got up and walked to the door, but both times I took her hand and led her back to bed.

Just when it seemed as if she was settling down, she started rocking herself back and forth, her arms wrapped around her torso, gently at first, and then harder and harder. She put her arms up in the air and started waving them around as if she was batting something away. Her eyes were closed, but she was making the guttural moaning sound again, and then with one super roll, she fell off the bed onto the floor. Bernie came rushing in, and I explained what had happened. He lifted her up and put her back in the bed. Although she was getting sleepy, thanks to the medication, the rocking resumed, and it was only a minute before she threw herself out of bed again.

Bernie and I had the same idea at the same time. I lifted her up, and he pulled out the trundle under the bed. At only about six inches off the floor, she wouldn't hurt herself if she fell out, and maybe, since she was accustomed to sleeping on a mattress on the floor, this would be more familiar to her. I laid her down again and covered her in the Hello Kitty quilt. Bernie kissed her goodnight, and I stayed with her another forty-five minutes until she was asleep. I left her bedroom door open and a nightlight in the hall so that if she did wake up, she could find us or we would hear her. Grabbing all of the poopy clothes and towels from the bathroom, I took them downstairs to the laundry room, closed the door, and then checked in on Willie, who had already checked out. We were all exhausted—physically, mentally, and emotionally. And it had only been half a day!

Back upstairs, I washed my face, brushed my teeth, and slipped into bed beside Bernie, who also looked sound asleep. The clock on my nightstand read 12:30 a.m. I remembered that tomorrow was Saturday, so I could sleep in until six.

As I lay on my back, looking at the ceiling, I replayed the day, thinking about what we could have done better, what we could do better tomorrow, how soon I could start toilet-training her, and how to keep her from swallowing the ocean water. I was setting myself up for a sleepless night, when Bernie reached across the bed and took my hand in his. I turned my head to peer at him. "That went well, don't you think?" He winked at me in the semi-darkness of our bedroom. I started laughing, he did, too, and we must have laughed for ten minutes. I'm sure we both fell asleep with smiles on our faces.

15

Ready, Set, Go

Day Two. I overslept until six-thirty and woke up with a start. Where was Danielle? And where was Bernie? I jumped out of bed and sprinted down the short hall between our bedroom and hers, then nearly tripped over my husband, who was sitting on the floor outside her door, watching her . . . sleep? She was lying on her back, the Hello Kitty comforter twisted around her waist and legs, her head propped on a pillow, snoring softly. I sat down across from Bernie and asked him how long he had been there. "Ten minutes. I didn't want to wake you. Look how peaceful she is."

"Don't wake her up!" I hissed at him, gesturing for him to come with me. He pulled her door partway shut, and we tiptoed to the kitchen to put coffee on and make breakfast. Ten minutes later, Willie came upstairs still rubbing sleep from his eyes, then did what millions of other American kids do on Saturday mornings—turned on the television to watch cartoons and flopped on the couch.

We didn't hear Danielle coming down the hall, but when I turned around to ask Willie if he wanted waffles or toast, there she was standing in the living room. Her hair—a little longer than chin length, fine but thick and cut in a bowl with bangs—looked like a fright wig. When she rocks in bed, she moves her head along with her body, twisting it from side to side on her pillow, which results in something atop her head that resembles a nest of twigs assembled by a blind bird. I couldn't help a laugh that escaped me, and when Bernie turned around, he did the same. Willie looked up from his cartoons long enough to state the obvious. "Her hair looks crazy!"

I took her by the hand to walk her to the bathroom, change her diaper, and try to get a brush through her hair. The diaper change was a breeze, the hair something else entirely. Danielle threw her arms around her head, jerked away, and started wailing and crying. I had barely touched her head with the brush. The commotion bought Bernie and Willie running down the hall and was so loud I was sure Bill and Doris could hear it from across the street.

What was the reason for her fear of anyone coming near her head? She had pulled away yesterday at the beach when Steven tried to pat her head, and now she was freaking out at the brush. All I could think is that someone—her mother, her brothers—must have hit Danielle around her head or at least pulled her hair. Something very real had caused this over-the-top reaction. But unless we elected to shave her head, which was not an option, we would have to figure out how to make brushing her hair less traumatic for her and for us.

We needed to simultaneously distract and comfort her. Bernie had already calmed her down quite a bit by simply picking her up and walking back and forth in the hall with her as you would a baby. She was just considerably larger than a baby, and her legs dangled below Bernie's knees. I thought we'd give it another shot, so we went back to her bedroom. I had Bernie sit on the bed across from Danielle, and I placed her so that her back was to the room, to me and the scary hairbrush. While he held her hands and played songs on the Lullaby Gloworm we got her, I approached her head from behind. A weed whacker would have been a better tool than a brush. As gently as I could, I started at the bottom, letting her know she was all right, that we were just going to brush out her hair to look pretty and it wouldn't take long. She wasn't completely on board with that, but rather than wailing, she whimpered, letting Bernie guide her hands to squeeze Gloworm to make him light up and play a song. When I was finished and her hair was smoothed out again, we both praised her profusely. Bernie took her to the bathroom to admire herself in the mirror, repeating over and over, "What a pretty girl! Look at pretty Danielle! Pretty, pretty girl!" That seemed to please her, or at least it didn't upset or annoy her, so he and I slapped five on another small victory and went to the kitchen for a celebratory coffee.

I called Willie and Danielle to come to breakfast, but when not even Willie answered, I looked into the living room. Danielle had plopped on the sofa beside him, her legs curled up under her like a pretzel and her upper body leaning against him. He looked at me with wide eyes as if to say, "Help!" She was fixated on the cartoons, so I turned off the television, pulled her up from the sofa, and led her to the kitchen, pointing out the blueberries she had liked so much the night before.

I repeated the word *blueberry* each time I gave her one. Then *strawberry* several times. Then I put them both on a plate and pointed to first one and named it, then to the other and named it. Blueberry. Strawberry. Blueberry is blue. Strawberry is red. In the five seconds it took me to get the chocolate milk out of the refrigerator, she crammed all of the remaining blueberries and strawberries into her mouth, her cheeks as fat as a nut-hoarding chipmunk. Lesson over.

I got Danielle's now clean clothes out of the dryer and brought them up to her room. I was curious whether she knew the first thing about dressing herself or was open to learning. I took her pajamas off and held a T-shirt in front of her. "Do you want to put your shirt on, Danielle?" Blank stare. "Do you want to help me put your shirt on?" She looked somewhere over my shoulder. "We have to get dressed to take the dogs for a walk. Don't you want to help me?" She turned her back. Guess not. "That's okay. I'll show you how, and we'll work on this another time." With her hair brushed and her dressed, I realized I had forgotten to brush her teeth last night, and I dug through the backpack. No toothbrush, but a very odd bathing suit. It was yellow with short sleeves and a high neck, with huge pads front and back. It looked like something a peewee football player would wear. "What is this, Danielle? Is this your bathing suit?"

I had decided that I was going to talk to her as if she could understand everything I said. That was how babies learned. Well before they themselves could talk, they absorbed all of the language around them. If they were never spoken to, how could they possibly learn to speak? I wasn't going to assume it was too late for Danielle to learn

Danielle playing bubbles with Mom.

or that because she couldn't talk to me, she didn't comprehend what I was saying. How would she ever feel like a part of our family if we didn't find some way to include her in everything?

I added a toothbrush to my shopping list, along with a hairbrush, clothes, a bathing suit, and sandals. The only shoes she had were big black clunkers that looked like boys' shoes and were hard to put on and take off a squirming child.

I got Willie and the dogs, and holding Danielle firmly by the hand, we made a short loop of the neighborhood, shouting hello to all of the people who were out working on their yards or washing their cars, but we didn't stop to chat. Bernie was in the driveway talking on the phone when we got back. "All right, Garet, thanks for calling. We're on our way to the store to pick up some things for her. We'll talk to you tomorrow." I asked him if anything was wrong. "No, she was just checking in, asking how Danielle was doing and how the visit was going." "What did you say?" "Great!"

On the way to Target, I wondered what Danielle's daily life was like in the foster home. I doubted that it was very similar to what we were doing, but she certainly didn't seem to be having any trouble adjusting. Her good mood changed the minute we got out of the car, and she saw that we were going into a store. She pulled away from Bernie's grip and made a dash for it in the parking lot, but she didn't get far before he grabbed her by the arm. He turned her to face him and very sternly told her she was not to do that. He pointed to a car driving slowly past and said how dangerous it was, that she could have been hurt. I was instantly thrust back to the times when each of my three boys pulled the same thing in a parking lot, darting out between cars in that one second while you're fiddling with the car seat or locking the door. It had scared me to death all three times. Each boy was still in diapers when he did it, which cushioned the quick smack on the bottom I instinctively gave him. Those are the only times I've ever been physical with any of my kids, and it sure got their attention. It must be an unwritten rite of childhood and parenthood. Danielle was also wearing diapers, but even a well-padded tap on the behind would not have been appropriate. We had no idea what she had been through and whether physical punishment had been part of her ordeal.

Bernie lifted her up and put her in the basket section of a cart, but her tantrum got worse when we got inside the store—wailing, screeching, hitting herself on the legs, and biting her own forearms. It was an arresting performance. I gave her the hairbrush and the tooth-brush I had picked out, hoping it would help her get familiarized with them, but she dropped both over the side of the cart onto the floor. People were staring, and Willie looked embarrassed. I told Bernie to take Willie with him to the auto department to take care of his list, while I wheeled the screaming meemie to grab up some clothes and a bathing suit, then zipped over to shoes. Danielle stopped cry-ing almost immediately and seemed to take an interest in a pair of pink slip-on sneakers I picked up. "What do you know?" I thought to myself. Just like a girl to be distracted by a cute pair of shoes.

We met Willie and Bernie at the cashier station, where Danielle started wailing again. Bernie carried her out, while I stayed inside to check out and took the opportunity to talk to Willie privately.

"You know, Danielle is going through a pretty big change right now. She is with an all-new family in an all-new place. She had no choice but to be here. She doesn't know what's going on from one minute to the next and has no way to tell us what she needs or wants. Her crying and yelling are the only ways she knows how to communicate, just like babies before they learn their words. But she also communicates with us when she laughs, when she smiles, when she sits beside you to watch cartoons, even when she steals your French fries."

Willie smiled at that. "She acts like a baby, but she's so much bigger than a baby. It's kind of weird."

I said, "Yes, it is, but that is a great way to look at it. She is like an overgrown baby. She missed so much when she was a baby and a toddler and a little girl. She is starting way behind everyone else. It's like starting a race after everyone else has almost gotten to the finish line. She has a lot of catching up to do, and she may never catch all of the people who started before her. But we have to let her try and help her along the way. It's the only way she will learn. There are times she will embarrass you, and I understand that and don't think badly of you for it. It's the people who are staring at her who should know better. Keep in mind that we will probably never see those people again, but, hopefully, Danielle will be with us forever."

Willie looked thoughtful. "Okay, Mom, thanks. Are we going to the beach after lunch?"

At the car, I put Danielle's new shoes on her, and Bernie made a big fuss about how pretty they were. I handed her the brush and the toothbrush to play with on the way home, and this time she held onto them. After lunch, I asked if she wanted to help me put her pretty new bathing suit on so we could go back to the beach. She didn't want to help, but she did allow me to put it on without a fuss.

Willie had brought pails and shovels to make sand castles, but Danielle had no interest in that at all. She just wanted to be in the water, splashing, rolling, and batting at the waves. She had no fear of putting her head underwater, which was amazing to me. I know people who have been around the beach their entire lives who won't go under the surface. The seaweed on the surface scared her at first, but when I took a piece and handed it to her, she seemed to like the texture of it and took to chasing it in the waves.

Out of the water, she tried walking on my feet so that she wouldn't have to touch the sand. We spend a lot of time at the beach when the weather is good, so we needed to get her over that particular phobia. Bernie picked her up, took her about ten feet away from the water, put her down, and walked quickly away to the edge of the water. The only way she could get to him was to walk over the sand. He called to her several times before she did it, but when she did it, I told her what a good girl she was and that if she did it three more times, Dad would give her a ride. Dad? Bernie and Willie looked at me. It had slipped out. I was so used to saying it to Willie, and how else should I refer to this new man in her life? Bernie? Mr. Lierow? Uncle Bernie? *Dad* was it. I wondered if Danielle even knew what the word meant. It had probably never been used in her presence.

After her fourth successful journey across the sand, Bernie/Dad picked her up and put her on his shoulders. Then he ran and turned in circles, with Danielle grasping his head, laughing out loud. Willie chased after them. We looked like any other family enjoying a day at the beach.

The Revenge of the Saltwater was especially severe after dinner, so bad, in fact, that I couldn't risk taking Danielle to walk the dogs, so I sent Bernie and Willie without us. The smart move would have been to just keep her on the toilet, but she was not cooperating. So I gave her some Kaopectate, then we read and played with her stuffed animals between explosions. By the time the boys and the dogs came back, she had been in the shower three times and had wiped out three outfits, three pillows, a comforter, and a rug. I put out her medication and handed her off to Bernie so I could take a shower. Naturally, she was a little angel for him. When I came back to the living room to tell her it was time for bed, she was already dozing off, sitting in his lap watching *Sponge Bob*, her head on his shoulder. Daddy's little girl.

Sunday morning I went in to wake Danielle and found her lying quietly in her bed, squeezing Lullaby Gloworm to make it sing. "Good morning, Sunshine! Let's get you changed." She had slept for nearly nine hours, so it wasn't surprising that she had wet through her diaper, pajamas, and sheets onto the plastic mattress cover. Before breakfast she had a shower, and I put on her new dress, since we were going to try church.

Danielle dressed for church.

We attended Beach Baptist, a small church with a membership that spanned the ages from infant to eighty, sometimes all in the same family. We loved the classes and the activities for kids. There was always something going on that Willie could participate in. The congregation was very committed to outreach service, and there were adult and youth Bible study classes on Wednesday nights following a fellowship meal.

Breakfast and Sunday school preceded Sunday service, but we decided not to press our luck and just to see how long Danielle might be able to sit in the chapel with us. Our church family was so close that everyone knew we had been to see Danielle and had been waiting for a home visit. The Sunday before this, people were asking if we had heard anything, and at that point, we hadn't. I couldn't wait to introduce Danielle to our pastor and his wife.

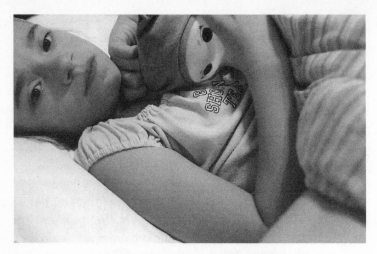

Danielle with the famous Lullaby Gloworm.

With all of the excitement of the last three days, I had completely forgotten that it was Palm Sunday. Standing at the top of the wide staircase that led to the entrance were some of the older teens, holding armfuls of palm fronds to hand out as people arrived. We all took one, including Danielle, although she promptly tried to put it in her mouth. The teens laughed, then were embarrassed for laughing. Bernie reassured them, "It's okay. This is Danielle. She is visiting with us this weekend. She does some funny things." Personally, I hadn't found the explosive eruptions the night before that amusing, but it was better to laugh than get upset over them.

From the foyer, we walked through the double doors into the sanctuary, and the people who were already seated glanced back to see who was coming in. Their smiles of recognition and hello turned to puzzlement when they saw Bernie holding Danielle's hand, then back to beaming smiles again when they realized who she was. For a second, I thought people were going to applaud, with palms waving in their clapping hands. I was struck thinking of the images we grew up with in the church, of Jesus entering Jerusalem on a donkey, and the residents laying down their cloaks and palms on the road before him.

People in several pews moved over to make room for us, and we chose the one closest to the rear. I knew Danielle wouldn't make it through the entire hour, and I wanted to be able to get out without disturbing the service.

The choir and the clergy proceeded in. The pastor, whose wife's interest in adoption had inspired us, reached out to pat Bernie's back as he walked past, then he beamed at us from the pulpit.

He welcomed everyone to Palm Sunday services and invited people to raise their palm fronds in the air. The palm branch, he said, is a symbol of triumph and victory. I smiled over Willie's and Danielle's heads at Bernie, thinking that God was sending us another message.

Less than ten minutes later, Danielle was sending a message loud and clear: I'm done. She began rocking, moaning, and making the woo-woo-woo sound again, so we made a hasty exit just as the choir stood to sing "Hosanna, Loud Hosanna." Danielle, Loud Danielle.

At home, she threw a major tantrum with real tears. All three of us tried to comfort her with no success until Willie went and fetched her Lullaby Gloworm, and that quieted the storm.

Bernie suggested that instead of the beach, we try the pool for an afternoon swim. I seconded the motion, thinking it would save me several trips to the shower and the washing machine. At lunch we discovered something else that Danielle loved as much as French fries: watermelon. I had cut hers into bite-size pieces, but one second of inattention cost Bernie his slice and then Willie his. Watermelon juice dripped down both sides of her mouth, making her look like a vampire who had just feasted on a particularly robust victim. From her mouth it dripped to her chest, her lap, and her legs, necessitating her second shower of the day before we could get into the pool.

It was an ordeal getting the "bathing suit" on Danielle that the foster family had sent, and when she and I walked out to the pool where Bernie and Willie were already swimming, they both laughed out loud. "She looks like the Michelin man!" Bernie kindly observed. "No!" Willie countered. "She looks like she's in one of those sumo wrestler costumes!" Any other girl would have been reduced to a puddle of tears by such humiliating commentary on her appearance in a bathing suit, but Danielle was blissfully unaware, focused on the hot tub. Completely unafraid, she lowered herself in using the rail and splashed happily at the bubbles. I asked Willie and Bernie to get in with her, although it wasn't deep enough to get her in any trouble, particularly with that ridiculous bathing suit. Willie showed her how to make a water tornado by running in circles, and she grasped the concept very quickly, laughing with delight at the swirling water. When she tired of that, she pulled herself out, walked two steps to the edge of the pool, and, before any of us could react, took one more step into the pool. "Danielle!" we yelled simultaneously. We needn't have worried. The suit didn't even let her head go under but kept her right at the surface, where she bobbed like a human buoy, not too happily. Danielle liked going underwater, and this was next to impossible in that suit. Still, I felt as if she needed something—it wouldn't do to have her drown under our watch—so I went to her room to get the new bathing suit we had bought the day before and changed her in the downstairs bathroom. "Look how pretty you are!" I said as I pointed to her image in the mirror. I got Willie's life jacket out of the storage box, snapped it on her, then watched as she ran to the pool and jumped in. The life jacket gave her just enough buoyancy to keep me from worrying and little enough that she could touch the bottom of the pool for a second or two when she jumped in, then bob back to the surface.

Jump. Bob. Get out. Jump. Bob. Get out. Each time Danielle got out and stood at the side of the pool, Bernie and Willie would

Danielle in the hot tub wearing the Michelin man
swimsuit the foster home sent with her.

say, "Ready, set, go!" The key word "Go!" roughly corresponded with
the moment she leaped into the water.

After about a dozen times, she hesitated, and I thought she
must be getting tired. Not exactly. I don't know whether it was
the repeated leaps into the pool or the tornado-making adventure
in the hot tub, but just as Willie and Bernie shouted "Go!" out of
Danielle's mouth came a stream of projectile vomit so forceful, it
shot like a fountain over at least half of the pool's surface, as well as
onto a horrified Bernie and Willie, who shouted, "Gross!" at the top
of his lungs. At first I thought the bright red vomit was blood, but
the pieces of watermelon floating all over the pool revealed its true
nature. Gross, indeed.

Willie dove deep and swam underwater to the other side of the
pool, checking himself for watermelon as he scooted up the ladder.
Bernie came through the vomit, while I grabbed Danielle up in
a towel and carried her inside, with Willie and Bernie on my heels.

I sent Willie into his bathroom to shower off, sent Bernie outside to hose off, and ran up the stairs with Danielle, who continued to spew watermelon vomit down the hallway to her bathroom. I was just hoping to get her in there before diarrhea hit again, which seemed inevitable, considering the amount of pool water she must have drunk. I sat her on the toilet with her Hello Kitty musical pillow while I peeled off my puke-covered clothes, washed my face, and put on the first thing I grabbed out of the dirty clothes hamper. Sure enough, what hadn't come out of her mouth was coming out the other end, but at least she was on the toilet. Progress!

As I took her off the toilet and put her into the shower, Bernie came in, phone to his ear.

"Yes, Garet, everything is still going great. We're having lots of fun. . . . We went to church this morning. . . . Today is Palm Sunday, you know. . . . It was really nice. . . . We only stayed about ten minutes, though. . . . Yes, she's sleeping well. She loves the room Diane made for her, it's very pink. That girl thing, Hello Kitty. . . . Really, she hates cats? Funny, she loves Hello Kitty. . . . She doesn't like shopping much. . . . . Yesterday, we went to Target to get her some clothes, what the foster family sent didn't fit. . . . Too big. We got her some shoes and a new bathing suit. That thing they sent her is crazy. . . . It's like a flotation device. . . . She didn't wear it to the beach. . . . Yes, twice. The first day she got here and yesterday, but she drank so much saltwater it gave her terrible diarrhea. She wiped out everything she had. . . . Today we tried the pool. We put her in her new suit and a life jacket, and she loved that because she could go under. She loves the water. . . . She's eating great. She must have eaten a quarter watermelon at lunch today. Unfortunately, it's all over our swimming pool right now. . . . Yeah. We've never seen such powerful projectile vomit. It was pretty impressive. . . . No, no worries. Diane has her in the shower right now. . . . We've been cleaning up one end or the other since we got her. . . . Yeah, it's pretty comical. . . . No big deal. She's sleeping pretty well. . . .

The rocking is less violent, and she only gets up two or three times. We just put her back in bed. I think she feels better with the door open so she can see the nightlight in the hall. . . . Willie's fine, thanks for asking. He's been great with her. . . . Yeah, he's a good kid. What time are we supposed to bring her back tomorrow?"

Here, there was a long silence on Bernie's end, and he had kind of a confused but happy look on his face as he listened to Garet. "Really? Are you sure? For how long? Really? That would be fantastic! . . . Sure, I'll check with her, but I'm sure it's okay. Just a minute." He pressed the phone onto his leg and told me Garet wanted to know if we could keep her several more days. "Really? Is she sure? How long? Can we have her all week?"

Bernie got back on the phone. "Diane wants to know if she can stay for the week. . . . Yes, we're sure. . . . Oh, really? That's funny. No, we'll keep her as long as we can. Sure, feel free to call in every day. . . . Yes, of course, I have your number. . . . Yes, we'll call if we need you. Thanks so much, Garet."

When he hung up, we beamed at each other. Neither of us had even talked about the fact that Danielle was supposed to go home the next day because it made us so sad. What a gift this was, to have her with us for the rest of the week. If we had known, I wouldn't have tried to cram so many activities into two days.

Taking Danielle out of the shower, Bernie told her the good news. "Sweetie, you're staying with us all week! " As he was saying it, she turned to face him and let go with another dose of water-melon vomit. I handed him a towel. "'We've not been cleaning up one end or the other since she got here, Bernie. *I've* been cleaning up one end or the other and everything in between. But thanks for offering. Here's a towel for her and one for you. I'm going to start dinner. When you're done with Danielle, she can watch cartoons with Willie while you clean out the pool. Thanks!"

Hoping not to stir up any more digestive issues for Danielle, I made breakfast for dinner, one of Bernie's and Willie's favorites.

We found out that Danielle loves pancakes but not scrambled eggs. After a long walk with the dogs after dinner, chats with the neighbors—who all remarked on what good color Danielle was getting—and a big kiss for the giant Easter bunny, Danielle watched an hour of Nickelodeon on the sofa with Willie and Bernie, while I put all of the watermelon-scented bathing suits and towels in the wash and cleaned up after dinner.

I was in the kitchen when Bernie called me to the living room with some sense of urgency. I was expecting another eruption, but instead, Bernie and Willie had huge smiles on their faces. "Listen to this, Diane." Bernie leaned close to Danielle and asked her if she was ready to go to bed. She didn't respond. "It's time to get ready for bed, Danielle. Remember. Ready, set, go!" She looked up at Bernie, and very softly she said, "Go."

I froze, dishtowel in hand, staring at her. "Do it again, Bernie," I urged. "Ready, set, go!" And from Danielle, "Go." Her voice was

Danielle at the Easter egg hunt, the Saturday before
Easter, on Bernie's shoulders.

flat, there was no inflection to the word like Bernie's, but she had said a word that we could understand.

Bernie picked Danielle up in his arms to carry her to her room. "Let's go," he said to her. "Go," she repeated as they turned the corner to the hall. Willie's eyes were on the television. I wondered if he felt any jealousy over the attention we were giving Danielle. "Willie, come out to the kitchen with me and tell me what to put in your lunch for tomorrow. I want you to know how proud Dad and I are of you. We know it's not easy bringing someone new into the family and especially someone like Danielle. You are being an amazing big brother, and we appreciate your help so much."

"Okay. Do I have to go to school tomorrow? I can help with Danielle."

"Nice try, Willie. Yes, you do have to go to school. I'll manage. Now go get ready for bed."

With Willie in school and Bernie at work, it was just Danielle and me, and I welcomed the opportunity for some alone time with her. She had already formed an attachment to Bernie, and Willie was her size. I felt a little bit like the odd man out, but I attributed that to her relating me—understandably so—with her mother. I would just have to overcome that.

Danielle let me hold her hand while we walked the dogs, but when I asked if she wanted to help and I put Cece's leash in her hand, she dropped it on the ground. Back at the house, we circled the perimeter of the backyard so I could point out all of the tropical plants and flowers, naming each one as we stopped. A butterfly hovered over one, and remembering what Garet had told us about her reaction to the butterflies painted on the hospital wall, I made sure Danielle saw it, naming that, too. I led her to the dock, careful to keep hold of her hand. I did not want to have to dive into the canal to fish her out, and who knew what digestive disaster might occur if she drank that water? It was a good morning for the manatee, and there were nearly two dozen of various sizes around the dock. Their odd shape and habit of surfacing, then disappearing again, piqued her interest, and her eyes followed them as they slowly swam about. I kept a running commentary, explaining what a manatee is, what they like to eat and do. I felt like I was talking to myself or at best to an infant, but I hoped Danielle was absorbing something.

I had chores to do, so I let her watch *Blues Clues* and *Sesame Street*—before turning off the television and directing her to her room to play. I checked on her several times. She liked to lie on her back on the floor or her bed and swing something over her head, usually a sock, and bat at it with her other hand. I didn't know what that represented or if it was something I should stop her from doing. Maybe I was reading a lot more into it, but I made a mental note to ask Mr. O'Keefe about it, then took the sock away and gave her one of her touch-tone toys to play with.

After lunch we went to the playground in the park, and we worked on her climbing up the slide's stairs by herself. Danielle figured out that once she got up to the top, she got to slide down. I thought this showed that she knew one thing could lead to another and that nothing we do is independent of the other. An ice cream truck came through the park, and I bought her a popsicle, but she didn't seem to like the cold. She put it in her mouth three or four times, trying it out, but finally dropped it onto the ground as if to show that she was done. I picked it up, put it in her hand, and walked her to the trash can, explaining all the while what we were doing and why. From the park we went to pick up Willie. I was going to take her into the school but decided that until we were sure, there was no sense introducing her to a bunch of new people. Plus, I didn't want to embarrass Willie. It was one thing to have Danielle screaming at Target or on the beach with complete strangers and quite another to be at Willie's school among his peers. We waited for him in the car rider line, with Danielle moaning softly and rocking in the backseat. She didn't really acknowledge Willie when he got in the car, which I think hurt his feelings a little bit. We were all going to have to go on patience medication.

While Willie did his homework, Danielle swam in the pool, although she kept trying to take her life preserver off. That was one battle I would not let her win, and I thought that maybe one day Bernie could test her swimming ability without a life jacket as long as he was in the water with her.

After dinner—add mashed potatoes to the small list of what Danielle won't eat—we walked the dogs, chatted with the neighbors, came home, got her showered and into pj's, then watched *Sponge Bob*. Danielle was very relaxed and laid back, and when I told her it was time for bed, she stretched out her arms to me for the first time, her signal to be picked up. I lay down with her on the lower mattress of the trundle bed and read *Brown Bear* and *Good Night Moon*. I kissed her goodnight, turned out the light, and watched her from the hall. She was rocking but not nearly as badly as she had been the last several nights. It had been a very good day.

The rest of the week was more of the same, with accomplishments, setbacks, and a few surprises. As Danielle became comfortable in our home, she explored more, and her favorite place to explore was the refrigerator. Every time she came into the kitchen, she opened the refrigerator door. She never took anything out; she just looked, transfixed by all of the food. On her fourth night with us, I woke up with a start to see a light shining from the kitchen. Danielle had opened the bottom freezer drawer and was standing barefoot in it, staring into the open double doors of the fridge. "Danielle?" She looked a bit startled but didn't move. I picked her up and carried her to the kitchen counter to feel her feet. They were freezing! I was relieved that I had come in when I did, because I had no idea how long she had been standing there or how long it takes to get frostbite. While I was rubbing her feet, Bernie woke up and came into the kitchen. "What's going on?" I told him how I had found her, and he cracked up. "It's not funny, Bernie!

She could have gotten frostbite! She was standing on the pork chop family pack!" Bernie tried, unsuccessfully, to stop laughing, but the more I said, the funnier he seemed to think it was. "Bernie, this is not something we want to encourage!" I huffed before I took her down the hall to bed.

Less amusing was my completely frustrated attempt to start potty training. I had never toilet-trained a girl, but I had heard that boys were easier, at least in teaching them to urinate in the toilet where they could make bubbles. I had heard of little girls with big brothers who had attempted standing up to pee, with the expected dismal results.

I thought it might help Danielle if I demonstrated, so when we were home alone during the day, I took her into the bathroom with me every time I had to go. I was deliberately drinking lots of water to provide many opportunities for observation. I explained what I was doing and told her that she could do it, too, and if she could, then she wouldn't have to wear diapers anymore. When she paid attention, she seemed amused but not particularly interested. After I got up, I sat her down and talked to her. Nothing would happen until I relented and let her stand up. Then she would pee down her legs and onto the floor.

I sensed some conscious, deliberate resistance, and although that would have been maddening in any other child, coming from Danielle it was in a strange way encouraging. At least, it showed me she was capable of thinking something through, even if that thought was to show me she would learn this on her timetable and not mine. You are not the boss of me!

Bernie took a half day off so he could have some one-on-one time with her. They went to the bank and the park, then came home and got me, and we went to McDonald's for chicken nuggets and fries. French fries seem to bring out the worst of her astonishing appetite. She makes such quick work of them. At home, she climbed up into the leather chair—the Daddy Bear chair—and threw up every fry she had inhaled, along with the chicken nuggets and the chocolate milk. Not pretty.

Another trip to the shower for Danielle, then a rest on the lounge by the pool while I did laundry and ironed. I told her she could take a swim before we went to pick up Willie, and she tried to undress herself, which was a first. I put her suit and life jacket on, and she tippy-toed to the pool. We had asked Mr. O'Keefe about that when we were in his classroom, and he said it was not uncommon in children like Danielle. She had never really been taught to walk and didn't have much opportunity to do so in her mother's house. I also wondered if it was a reaction to being bare-foot on those disgusting bug-, feces-, and food-encrusted floors. I wouldn't want to touch them either.

But she needed to learn to walk normally, or her calf muscles would tighten. "Flat feet!" I reminded her, as we had seen Mr. O'Keefe and his aides do in the classroom, and she lowered her heels, then jumped into the pool, content to splash around with the pool toys by herself. When I told her it was time to come out, I anticipated the usual—she would swim away and I would have to go at least partway in to pull her out. On this day, she willingly came to the end with the steps, walked out on her own, and tried to take her life jacket off by herself. I helped her out of it, then waited to see what she would do next. She grabbed a towel but seemed unsure of how to manage it. I wrapped her up tight, telling her over and over what a good, smart girl she was to do all that by herself!

Upstairs, she started to run around, and I told her she had to get dried and dressed first, then waited again to see what she would do. She went into the bathroom, knowing the next step was for me to peel off her wet suit. I asked her if she wanted to sit on the potty, but instead, she walked naked to her bedroom, ready for a pull-up diaper and clothes. I couldn't wait to tell Bernie, so, while she played with her stuffed animals, I called him on his cell, giving him a play-by-play. He was so quiet, I thought the call had been dropped. "Bernie?" He was so moved, he couldn't speak for a minute. And so excited that on the way home, he stopped at a toy store and bought Willie a new kit to make miniature furniture and a toy for Danielle that said "Peek-A-Boo!" when you pushed a certain button. Using towels and blankets, Willie had been playing peek-a-boo with her all week, making her giggle, so she was familiar with the words and loved pushing the button over and over again. I was pretty sure that within a day or so, I would be wishing the Peek-A-Boo game would go away.

Willie was off for Good Friday, so we had a lazy day by the pool and then went to the park. Bernie and I were aware that the end of Danielle's visit with us was near, and we just wanted to be together as a family and enjoy the last couple of days together.

Since we would have to take her back on Easter Sunday, we decided to try the community Easter egg hunt at the Bay Oaks recreation center on Saturday.

There was no "special needs" category, and she had to go out with her age group, which was like sending a one-year-old out with eight-year-olds. Willie stuck close by her, but she was completely lost and, of course, didn't pick up a single egg. I was surprised that she held onto her basket. When it was over and Willie had a basket full of eggs, we tried a little tutorial. Willie put some eggs on the ground in front of her, and Bernie would guide her hand to the eggs, then guide her hand to the basket, and drop the eggs in. I opened an egg for her, unwrapped the chocolate candy, and put it in her mouth. Candy. Mmm. Good. Mmm. More. Mmm. Except that she didn't know how or really care to take the wrapper off the candy but just stuck it in her mouth.

The hunt was staged in a very open space, and as soon we picked the foil off Danielle's teeth, she took off running. She ran and ran, loving every minute of it. The area was fenced, so we could let her run as free as she wanted, and we didn't have to worry.

I thought that after all of those years of being confined to one room and never allowed outside, she must love to run.

That night, we ate dinner on the deck, walked the dogs, and took her to see Dorothy and Paul and Doris and Bill. Bernie held Danielle up to give Mr. Bunny a kiss good-bye. Everyone was getting sad, but we tried to hide it as best we could. We didn't want Danielle to pick up on our feelings.

Bernie changed her and put her in her pajamas, I popped some popcorn, and we huddled up on the sofa to watch *Happy Feet*. Danielle fell asleep on Bernie's lap, and when the movie ended, he carried her into her room, laid her gently on her bed, and tucked her Hello Kitty comforter around her.

Easter morning I woke up with a feeling of dread, and it took me a second to remember why. We were taking Danielle back to Tampa. I knew she had no idea what Easter was, but I felt like she was being cheated out of another holiday. I vowed that when she came back with us, we would celebrate every one as if it were her first. In fact, each would be her first. I wondered if she had ever had a birthday cake, much less a party.

I had hidden the Easter baskets the night before, in case Willie got up before me. He was at that age where he no longer really believed in the Easter Bunny, the Tooth Fairy, or Santa Claus, but he wasn't quite ready to let go of that part of his childhood and was afraid of the finality of saying it out loud.

When Willie did come upstairs, it wasn't with his usual enthusiasm. We were all feeling the weight of the pending separation. I asked him if the Easter Bunny had come, and he looked at me with the saddest face and told me he didn't know. "Can I get Danielle up, and we can look together?"

We went back to her room where she was playing on her bed with her Peek-A-Boo toy, and after I changed her, Willie took her by the hand and led her around the house until they found the baskets. The Easter Bunny had left Danielle a pink stuffed bunny in her basket, which she tried to eat, sticking an entire ear in her mouth.

Leave it to Danielle to make us all laugh. I told her the bunny was not for eating but that I had her favorite—waffles—for breakfast. She ate four—including half of one on Willie's plate that she snatched when he wasn't looking. I think he appeared distracted on purpose just to give her the opportunity.

I had washed all of the clothes the foster parents had sent and packed them into her bag, but I dressed Danielle in one of the outfits we bought her. I irrationally thought that it would offer her some type of protection as we sent her back into the unknown, or it would be a reminder of us. I asked her to sit on the potty one more time before we got in the car to go for the long drive back. She complied, although she didn't do anything but sit. She also didn't pee on the floor when she got up, so that was a plus.

Willie had loaded the backseat with toys again, Bernie carried out Danielle's little bag, and I made sure she had her pink bunny before we got in the car, drove off the island, and headed north toward Tampa.

The drive back was so different from the one a week earlier when we were bringing her home. We tried our best to stay cheerful and positive, but it was really hard. Who knew what Danielle understood about what was happening? And what difference would it have made? There was nothing any of us could do about it. Maybe it was best if she didn't understand, but she knew something was up. The farther north we drove, the more anxious she became, rocking more vigorously and moaning more loudly. Willie tried to distract her, but not even Lullaby Gloworm or Peek-A-Boo worked. That made it even harder on us.

We stopped at the McDonald's in Venice for lunch, and I was careful to monitor her fry intake. I didn't want the foster family to accuse us of making Danielle sick. It was pretty pitiful to be eating at McDonald's on Easter Sunday.

We had been told to meet the foster father in a Winn-Dixie parking lot. I wanted to take Danielle back to her home so we could see it and maybe talk to the foster mother, to let her know how Danielle had done. But they insisted on the parking lot. Bernie parked toward the back of the lot, as we had been asked to do, and we all got out of the car to wait. Willie and Danielle pulled on the Slinky, while Bernie and I watched, and I struggled to hold back my tears. Bernie told me later that he just wanted to grab her, get in the car, and drive away as fast as he could.

A few minutes later a black car with tinted windows pulled up beside our car, and the driver's side window eased down. "Are you the Lierows?" a man asked. "Are you Danielle's foster father?" we responded. He said he was and got out of the car, though he left it running. He called Danielle's name, but she did not respond. Bernie walked over, took the Slinky from Willie, and told him to tell Danielle good-bye. Willie gave her a big hug, which she allowed, although she did not reciprocate. I handed the foster father her bag and tried to tell him how well she had done last week, but he was uninterested in chatting. "My wife is holding Easter dinner, we've got to go," he said, making an obvious check of his watch. Bernie and I both kneeled down in front of Danielle. We told her how much we loved having her in our house and as part of our family. We promised her that we would be back for her soon, very soon. Then we kissed her, and they were gone.

We stood in the parking lot for another five minutes, hoping that by some miracle the Mercedes would come back, the foster father would tell us it had all been a terrible mistake, and Danielle would go home with us. That didn't happen.

The drive back was horrible. Willie played with the Peek-A-Boo toy and cried softly in the backseat before blurting out the classic children's lament: "It's not fair!"

No, I said, it isn't fair. Not a bit of it. Not what her mother had done, not what the DCF had done, not what was happening today.

I couldn't imagine the contrast between the life she was leaving behind at our house and what she was returning to—solitary confinement in a bedroom stripped of everything but a mattress and sheets. How confusing that must be to her, to be given a beautiful new life with people who loved her, only to have it snatched away.

When we got home, I went to Danielle's room, sat on the Hello Kitty comforter, hugged Lullaby Gloworm, and wept.

It's one thing to send your child off to college or her first apartment. It's a hard but natural transition understood by both parties. This was nothing of the kind. What did Danielle understand? Was she wondering if she had done something wrong? It would break my heart if she thought we were rejecting her, that we didn't want her. I hoped that somewhere deep inside she knew we were coming back, just as I believed she had somehow known we were coming for her in the first place.

Bernie came in the room, sat down on the bed, and put his arm around me. "I'll call Garet first thing in the morning to see how soon she can come back. Now let's get Willie and take the dogs for a walk." I told him to go on without me. I didn't think I could bear the questions about her from our neighbors. In such a short amount of time, she had become a member not only of our family, but of our community, and I knew everyone would be curious about how the exchange went in Tampa. Instead, I straightened up her room and put her stuffed animals and toys back in their places to wait for her, just as we would be waiting.

That night while lying in bed, I prayed to God to watch over Danielle until we could bring her home.

16

One Step Backward

One of my first thoughts when I open my eyes every morning and reach a level of coherency is "Where are my children?" I do a quick mental check, starting with our oldest, Shawn, and ending with Willie. The morning after we took Danielle back to Tampa, she increased my list from five to six. I didn't need to carry her for nine months, give birth to her, or share her DNA. She was our daughter, and leaving her with someone we didn't know felt as unnatural and wrong as if one of our boys had been taken away to be raised by another family.

I nudged Bernie. "When can you call Garet?" He opened one eye to look at the clock on his nightstand. "Diane, it's 5 a.m. I think we should wait until she gets into the office, don't you?" When he did call Garet before he left for work, he got voice mail on her cell and office phones. "Call me as soon as you hear!" I hollered after him on his way out the door.

An hour later he called and told me that he had confirmed to Garet that we wanted to adopt Danielle—as if there was a question—but that she said she would have to get back to us on what the next steps were.

The house was so quiet, the day so long without Danielle in it. I avoided her end of the hallway and got weepy all over again when I found one of her sippy cups behind the sofa. Every time I looked at the clock, I thought about what she might be doing at that moment. Was she on the swing, at lunch, listening to a story? Was she having a tantrum? Was she laughing? Was she stealing someone's sandwich?

I was surprised when Bernie came home for lunch, but he knew I was having a tough time being at home alone. Bernie is so sensitive to my moods and feelings, it never ceases to amaze me or make me grateful that after two strikes on both of our marital histories, we hit a home run when we found each other.

I asked if he thought it would be okay to call Danielle's school and check in with Mr. O'Keefe or Ms. Perez to see how she was doing. He smiled and told me he had already thought of that. While I was making him a sandwich, he called. He talked to the school secretary for a few minutes, then asked for Mr. O'Keefe but got Ms. Perez, who was in the main office.

As Bernie listened to her, he began to smile. I practically had my ear against his, trying to hear what she was saying, but he pushed me away. Then he gave Ms. Perez a recap of what we had done while Danielle was with us. "Yes, we were very busy," he laughed. "We had a ball. We're waiting to hear back from Garet White on what the next step is and when we can pick her up again. . . . Great, that's very nice of you. Yes, please tell Mr. O'Keefe hello and give Danielle a big hug from us. Thank you."

"What did she say? What were you smiling at? How is Danielle?" I peppered him with questions the way Willie does to me on a particularly hyper day. Ms. Perez had already been by the classroom twice to see Danielle and talk to Mr. O'Keefe. She said that no one could believe what a good mood Danielle was in. Mr. O'Keefe told Ms. Perez that she was a different child—happy, stimulated, and actively listening. They wanted to know what we had done to her!

All that we had done was love her, hug her, pay attention to her, and include her. All that we had done was what any normal parent would have done every day of her life. If just one week could make that much difference, I said to Bernie, just think what a month or a year might bring.

Knowing Danielle was happy made me feel so much better that I was able to go into her room, straighten it up, and strip the bed to launder everything for the next time she came to stay with us.

On my way to pick up Willie from school, I went to the drug-store to get the photos from her visit. At home, Willie and I went through them, laughing at Danielle in the hot tub with her sumo wrestler bathing suit, sitting on her bed with the stuffed animals, and, especially, kissing the giant inflated Easter bunny. I suggested that Willie draw a big picture about her time with us. I wrote a short note that Mr. O'Keefe could read to her, and put the draw-ing and the note in an envelope with some of the photos to mail to Danielle the next day.

The happy mood was short-lived. The minute Bernie walked in the door from work, I sensed that something was terribly wrong. It was confirmed by those four awful words everyone hates to hear: "We need to talk."

We knew that Michelle Crockett had appealed the termination of parental rights as soon as the ruling was made back in September 2006. It had been delayed and extended several times, but it was everyone's opinion that the TPR would not be overturned, and that there was no way on God's earth that Danielle would ever be returned to Michelle Crockett.

When we confirmed to Garet that we wanted to adopt, instead of being greeted by the DCF and the state and the legal system with support, help, and maybe even a bit of gratitude for taking one very needy child out of the system and into a family, we instead encountered yet another series of roadblocks, obstacles, and contradictions, all wrapped up tight in red tape.

It was so confusing that Bernie had taken notes, which did not necessarily clear things up because even under the best of circumstances his scribble was barely legible. This was the worst of circumstances, and it was nearly impossible to explain the inexplicable.

HKI's policy was that if there is an appeal pending on a child, he or she cannot be placed for adoption. Danielle had been allowed to visit with us to confirm our desire to adopt her—even though the appeal was pending—but once we confirmed that yes, we did want to adopt her, then she could not be placed with us as adoptive parents. My temples were starting to throb.

She could be placed with a foster family whose intent was to adopt her, but she could not be "placed for adoption."

Although we had jumped through every hoop, answered hundreds of questions, been investigated, screened, and interviewed, taken a ten-week series of classes, and paid a good amount of money to have a private agency do our Home Study so that we could be approved as an adoptive home, we were not set up as a foster home. That was an entirely separate license.

As long as Michelle Crockett's appeal was still pending, the only way that Danielle could come into our home again was for us to go back to our local agency to get our foster care license. We would not have to go through all of the testing that we did to be approved as an adoptive home, but there would be lots of paperwork. And it would take time, as any encounter with a government agency does.

But the worst news was the conflict between the two counties—Lee County, where we live, and Hillsborough County, where Danielle lived and under whose jurisdiction she was. Though it seems ridiculous and counterproductive, protocol and policy vary from county to county in the same state, and Lee and Hillsborough counties were pretty far apart.

Hillsborough County would allow nonrelative placement only if we had a foster license. Lee County would allow us to go to a judge and request an emergency nonrelative placement without a foster license, but Garet told Bernie that because Danielle was in a foster home in Hillsborough County and she was being cared for and there had been no complaints filed, there was no "emergency."

I was crying tears of frustration and practically sputtering with anger. It was so ridiculous and incomprehensible, especially when everyone kept telling us there was no way Michelle Crockett would ever get Danielle back. But she wouldn't let Danielle go. It was as if she was lashing out to say that if she couldn't have Danielle, she would make it as hard as possible for anyone else to have this child. If only she had fought half this hard for her daughter when she had Danielle, our little girl wouldn't be where she was now.

I asked Bernie if he thought they were trying to get us to give up. "We're not giving up, Diane. This is a setback, that's all. We know she will be with us sooner or later. I hate that it looks like it will be later, but she will be back. Why don't you call the DCF tomorrow and find out what we need to do to get our license? I'll stay in touch with Mr. O'Keefe and Ms. Perez so we can keep up with how Danielle is doing."

Bernie was right, of course. The only thing we could do was fight for her and have faith. The fighting part was easy. Bernie and I have always been scrappy and stubborn. And we were people of strong faith, but having faith in the DCF to do the right thing was a bit of a challenge. For the first time in my life, I fully understood the term "fighting the system," and I could see how people would just give up. But giving up was not in Bernie's or my DNA.

The next day I called the Florida Baptist Children's Home because it was our licensing agency and the place where we had taken our classes. I explained what we needed from Florida Baptist, and the agent took some information over the phone and said she would send me the paperwork. "How long does it typically take to get the license?" I asked. "We can't say. We have a lot of applications, and then it has to be routed through this office. It should be faster since you already have a Home Study, but I just can't say."

I told her I would come down that afternoon to pick up the forms. I didn't trust her to put them in the mail that day or even that week, and I didn't want to waste any more time. Before I picked up Willie from school, I went to Florida Baptist and got the thick envelope.

Bernie and I filled out everything that night, and I returned the paperwork to the agency the next day, making sure that it went directly to the woman I had spoken with. I considered sending a pie or a gift card to Nordstrom's along with it, but Bernie had given me that look when I mentioned it, so I skipped the bribes and just dropped off the papers. I hoped that the agency worker would see how desperate I was and take it upon herself to expedite our papers.

From there, I turned it over to Bernie Bulldog. If this woman thought I was a pain in the neck, wait until she started getting a call from Bernie every morning. I knew from experience that she would eventually do anything to send him away.

Either the agency worker's hands were tied, or Bernie's badgering didn't bother her. The wait dragged on. Willie said a prayer for Danielle every night at bedtime, and I thought of her during the day every day. Did she think we had forgotten her? Had she forgotten us? Each time Bernie talked to Mr. O'Keefe or Ms. Perez, they asked him what was taking so long, and it was clear that they were worried, too. Mr. O'Keefe was hesitant to speak negatively or say anything that might imply that the foster home was not helping Danielle, but Ms. Perez was forthright. She told Bernie that every week that went by, Danielle was moving backward, regressing to the child she had been when she first came to Sanders. Hearing that was at once heartbreaking and infuriating.

Finally, six weeks after we applied, six weeks after Danielle had been in our home, Bernie was told by Baptist that all of the paperwork for our license had gone through all of the channels, across all of the desks, and gotten all of the bureaucratic signatures required. We were approved. Now all that we needed was the actual paper license. I again offered to pick it up, but the agency worker told us it was in the mail. Bernie called Garet to tell her, and she said she would take it from there.

Almost a week later, we still hadn't gotten our license. At nearly ten on a Saturday night in late May, Willie was in bed, and Bernie and I were being couch potatoes watching a movie when his cell phone rang. He looked at the number and sat straight up. "Garet? What's going on? What? Tonight? Hold on." He held the phone to his chest and told me that Sanders Elementary had made a report the day before of suspicion of neglect due to a distinct downturn in Danielle's personal hygiene. They said she was coming to school every day smelling strongly of urine, that her clothes were not clean, and her hair was dirty. Danielle was still in diapers, so she had to be showered at least once a day, or she would reek. The school was obligated by law to report any suspicion of neglect or abuse.

Since finding out about the report late in the afternoon the day before, Garet had been working feverishly to complete the paperwork to have Danielle removed from the home. This was taken care of, but there was nowhere to place her in Hillsborough County. Because Garet knew we had been approved for a foster license, and because this would be considered a nonrelative emergency placement, all of the bases were covered. At least, we hoped so.

Garet wanted to know if we could come that night. I pointed out that it would be nearly two in the morning before we could get there. Bernie went back to Garet on the phone. "Do you think she is in immediate danger? If we leave here first thing in the morning, we can be there by ten. Where should we meet him? Okay. Yes, we'll call you tomorrow. Thank you, Garet."

We might as well have left the house then, because neither of us could sleep. But I didn't want to wake up Willie, and we needed time to take care of the dogs if we would be gone a full day. As good a sport as Dorothy was, I couldn't disturb her in the middle of the night.

We were on the road to Tampa at seven, with Bernie driving like a bat out of hell. Willie had loaded up the backseat with a Hello Kitty pillow, Lullaby Gloworm, the pink Slinky, the Peek-A-Boo toy, and about a half-dozen stuffed animals. There was barely room for him; I didn't know where we would put Danielle.

Garet told Bernie that Mr. Morgan would meet us with Danielle at 10 a.m. in the Winn-Dixie parking lot. We got there about 9:45. By 10:30, he still wasn't there. We called the foster home and the foster mother's cell phone and got voice mail at each. Garet had told us that they were members of a church close to the Winn-Dixie, where they supposedly took Danielle every Sunday. We went to two churches before we found it. Service was over, but we found the pastor and asked about the foster parents. He confirmed that they were members but said they hadn't been to church in more than a year. He called the numbers he had and left messages as well.

We went back to the parking lot, thinking that maybe the foster father had shown up, but he wasn't there and no one had called us back. Bernie remembered that the man ran a towing company, so while I stayed in the parking lot with Willie, Bernie went off to find a service station that might know of him. Sure enough, the workers there did, and Bernie asked them to call him, knowing that he would answer a call for a job. When the foster father answered, the attendant handed the phone to Bernie. Bernie was mad, but he was more fearful for Danielle, so he didn't want to cause any trouble. Danielle's foster father told Bernie that they'd had a hard time getting Danielle up that morning, but that as soon as his wife packed up all of her things, Mr. Morgan would be at the Winn-Dixie.

The three of us were standing beside our car when he pulled up beside us an hour later. He got out of his Mercedes, barely said hello, then opened the rear door.

I could not stop myself from gasping out loud. I felt as if someone had punched me in the stomach. Willie looked confused, and Bernie was just plain angry. Danielle was sitting alone. She didn't try to get out of the car but sat passively, staring straight ahead. Drooling, her tongue out one side of her mouth, she was so lethargic I was sure that her drug dosage had been increased. When she finally turned her head to look at us, I gasped again. The left side of her face was covered with scratches, one of them still bleeding slightly. Bernie pushed past the foster father to unbuckle Danielle and lift her up in his arms, which is when I saw more scratches on both arms.

I asked the foster father what had happened, how did she get the scratches? First, he told us she must have fallen on the playground because she came home from school that way on Friday. When I pointed out that one scratch was still bleeding, he said that she was playing outside that morning and fell again.

Neither scenario was likely. If she had fallen in school and gotten scratched that badly, the office would have called the foster mother and not simply sent Danielle home like that. And Garet would have mentioned it when she called and told us about the report the school had made. All that she had told us about was the personal hygiene problem. The scratches were sideways, from Danielle's ear across her cheek to her nose. They didn't look like they had come from a fall but from a person or an animal.

The foster father handed me a duffle bag with "her stuff," as he put it. All that Danielle had accumulated in almost nine years of life was in a canvas bag two feet long and a foot around. We had more of her things in the backseat of our car than what she had left her mother's home with—a soaking diaper—or what the foster family cleared out of her bedroom. The foster father did not attempt to touch Danielle or tell her good-bye but got in his car and drove away. He didn't look back.

Bernie buckled Danielle into the backseat of our car. I told Willie to get up front. I wanted to sit with her for awhile. I got an antiseptic wipe from the first aid kit we keep in the car and gently wiped her cheek and then her arms, telling her over and over how sorry we were that she got hurt, how sorry we were that it took so long to get her back, how much we missed her, and how happy we were to see her. She did not acknowledge me in any way, not even when I pushed the button to make her favorite toy say Peek-A-Boo.

We stopped at the McDonald's in Venice, and just like the first time when we brought her home, she had soaked through her diaper and clothes and onto the backseat. I dug through the duffle bag for dry clothes and found the outfit I had dressed her in on Easter Sunday. I also found the pink bunny that was in her Easter basket and handed it to her. Danielle didn't react, but she did hold onto it. After changing her in the restroom, I put the too-big shorts and the stained shirt in the trash. She wouldn't need them anymore.

The boys were waiting eagerly at the table for us. Willie had spread her fries on a tray and had already cut her burger into bite-size pieces. "Look, Danielle, your favorite! French fries!" He held one up and waved it before her. She didn't take it, and Willie looked like he was going to cry. "What's wrong? Doesn't she remember us?"

Bernie explained that it might take a while for her to be comfortable with us again. "Is she mad at us?" Maybe not mad, but definitely confused and hurt. No matter what the truth was or the reason why, we had let her down, and we would have to earn her trust all over again.

When we crossed the bridge onto Estero Island, Bernie made the first left he could for beach access parking. He picked Danielle up out of the backseat and carried her across the sand, then took off her sandals—the pink ones we had bought her—and set her gently down. Willie came to her side, clasped her hand in his, and led her to the water. She didn't resist. They waded into the sunset over the gulf, waves breaking at their knees, two small hand-in-hand silhouettes against the sinking sun in a brilliant red sky, ablaze with the promise of a glorious tomorrow. I had never seen anything more beautiful.

Bernie put an arm around my shoulder and squeezed tight. "It's going to be all right, Diane." I knew in my heart he was right. Danielle was home now, where she belonged, and we would never let her go again.

17

Two Steps Ahead

The first night that Danielle was back with us, she was so restless and rocked so violently that I stayed in her room with her until she fell into a fitful sleep. She got up three times during the night, and Bernie and I took turns redirecting her back to bed. It reminded me of when Willie was an infant.

We awoke at 5 a.m. to loud moaning from her room, where we found her up and pacing. She would not respond to my verbal requests to change her soaked diaper, so Bernie picked her up and carried her like a baby into the bathroom, where I struggled to get her into the shower. We had all been too tired to shower the night before, and she was definitely in need of some "personal hygiene." Brushing her hair was out of the question. I wondered how Mrs. Morgan had done it. Did someone hold Danielle's hands and let her scream while another person pulled out the tangles and the knots?

Bernie took the morning off to give me a hand and make calls to Garet and Mr. O'Keefe. I drove Willie to school to give Bernie some time with Danielle, and when I came back, she was sitting on his lap at the kitchen table, letting him feed her pieces of banana. That was a start. He told me her medication was low, so he asked me to call the pharmacy for refills, and he would pick it up on the way home from work.

He called Sanders Elementary first to let them know we had Danielle and that because there was less than a week of school left, she would likely not be back. The office put him through to Mr. O'Keefe, and Bernie told him that we had picked Danielle up yesterday from the foster father and asked him about the scratches. Mr. O'Keefe had no idea what Bernie was talking about and said that it had to have happened after Danielle left the school on Friday, which was exactly what we suspected.

They chatted about Danielle's progress in the last year, and Mr. O'Keefe said that the school year evaluations would be in the office by the end of the week. He told Bernie to feel free to call him with any questions. It was probably a mistake to leave a door open like that for Bernie; he would be calling Mr. O'Keefe once a week.

Bernie thanked Mr. O'Keefe and Ms. Perez for caring so compassionately for Danielle and providing her with a safe place to be. "Garet said that the school and your classroom were her sanctuary, the one place she felt safe and loved. We are so grateful to you and Ms. Perez." Before Bernie hung up, he promised to let Mr. O'Keefe know how the adoption was proceeding.

Bernie called Garet next and filled her in on yesterday's adventure with Mr. Morgan, on Danielle's state of mind, and on her withdrawal from us. "Physically, she seems fine except for the scratches. . . . The ones on her face and arms. . . . We don't know, we thought you might know. . . . Mr. Morgan told us two versions, that it happened at school and that it happened playing outside at home when she fell. I just talked to Mr. O'Keefe, and he said she was fine when she left Friday, no scratches. It looks to us like someone did it to her. . . . Okay. . . . We will. . . . Okay. . . . When will that come? We'll do that right away. We also need to get her medication refilled, it's almost gone. . . . Alright, we'll talk tomorrow. Thanks, Garet."

Garet told Bernie that we needed to take pictures of Danielle and the scratches and fax them to her so that she could include them in the report about why Danielle was removed from the foster home and put in an emergency placement. At the same time, Garet was faxing us a letter from HKI naming us as caregivers "authorized to consent to the child's ordinary and routine medical and educational needs." We had to take her to a doctor to get a physical within twenty-four hours of her coming to our home so that the doctor could attest to her condition in case anything ever came up later.

That didn't leave us much time. First, we needed to take photos of Danielle's face and arms, so I sat with her squirming on my lap on the floor of her room while Bernie got some close-ups. Garet was faxing the authorization letter to the business office of the contractor Bernie was working with that week, so I thought we would run and pick that up, drop the film at a one-hour photo place, take Danielle to a walk-in clinic for a checkup, pick up the photos, and fax copies to Garet from the office, all before we had to pick up Willie from school.

The doctor's office was crowded, and the wait seemed interminable, especially for an eight-year-old girl who did not want to be there and the adults who were trying to calm her. Danielle threw one heck of a tantrum. Though she had never been to a doctor during the first seven years of her life, she'd had plenty of experience with them in the last two. Her histrionics caused all of the other moms in the waiting room to pull their children close to them, as if Danielle would hurt them. Mr. O'Keefe and Ms. Perez had both told us that Danielle had never once been aggressive with another child. She had never hit, struck out, or bitten any of her schoolmates, even when she had been on the receiving end of the same. Mr. O'Keefe said Danielle had always been very sweet-natured. At the moment, though, she was acting more like the little girl in *The Exorcist* than the one in *Nell*. When the nurse came out to call back a child who had been there before us, her mother gave us her spot. It was very kind of her, and I'm sure all of the other people in the waiting room thanked her profusely once we left them in peace.

The tantrum worsened in the even smaller examining room. Bernie picked Danielle up and walked her back and forth, just as he had when Willie was an infant and inconsolable. Finally, the doctor knocked rather tentatively on the door and came in with a nurse. "What have we here?"

I wouldn't have known where to begin to answer that question, although we gave the doctor a brief synopsis and told him why she needed the check-up. He was very kind and soothing, and Danielle settled down a bit. He let her look at his stethoscope before he listened to her heart, and she immediately put that part in her mouth. Same with the light that shines in the ear and the rubber hammer that tests for reflexes. The one thing that was supposed to go in her mouth—the thermometer—she kept pushing out with her tongue. Finally, the doctor put his palm to her forehead and proclaimed, "98.6! Perfectly normal!" Bernie and I couldn't help it, we both started laughing. There Danielle was, her uncombed hair sticking out every which way, wearing a diaper, rocking and moaning and reaching for the doctor's stethoscope to put the microphone end in her mouth. *Normal* was not exactly the first word that came to mind. The doctor and the nurse joined in, and seeing us all laughing brought a tiny smile to Danielle's face.

The doctor reached out as if to pat her head, and Bernie and I shouted simultaneously, "Don't touch her head!" The doctor jerked his hand back as if he had touched a hot stove, and we starting laughing again. Overall, he pronounced her in good health, noting no marks except for the scratches.

We barely had time to get the photos and fax them and the doctor's report to Garet before school dismissed and we had to pick up

Willie. It was the last full week before summer vacation. All of the year-end testing was done, so the kids were just playing and having parties, which meant there was no homework, a relief to Willie and me. It also meant that Willie was a bit more hyper than usual, thanks to all of the sugar at the parties. At home, I put Danielle in her bathing suit and life jacket, and while she, Bernie, and Willie played in the pool, I made dinner.

I had decided that we weren't going to do anything special or different until Danielle was settled back into our routine and felt safe and secure. I was still worried about all of the paperwork and the legalities, and I couldn't feel confident that Michelle Crockett wasn't somehow going to get Danielle back. It seemed safest and wisest to stick close to home.

We had grilled chicken for dinner—two legs for Danielle, baked potatoes, and salad—then went on the evening dog walk. People out on the streets and in their yards made a big fuss over Danielle. She seemed wary but not frightened. We found Dorothy, who gave Danielle a big hug, got her to pet Amber, and invited us to dinner the next night. When we came to Doris and Bill's corner, Danielle stopped at the edge of their yard, looking at the place where the bunny had been. Bernie nudged me in the ribs. "Look, she remembers the bunny. She's looking for him. That's good!" He was right, it was good. Danielle had made connections while she was with us, and she remembered something, even if it was a blow-up bunny.

At home, after Danielle was showered and in her pajamas, I took out the photos from her visit with us at Easter and sat at the kitchen table with her in my lap. We ate blueberries and looked at the pictures, one by one—the beach, the pool, her room, and the dogs. Each one I named, hoping she might repeat a word back to me. Danielle was silent, but when I showed her the photo of Bernie holding her up to the inflatable bunny so she could kiss its cheek, she reached out her hand and patted the bunny. I kissed her on the cheek and squeezed her tight. She didn't pull away.

When it was time for bed, I realized I had forgotten to call in for the refill for Danielle's medication. There was only enough left for tomorrow morning. I put a Post-it note on the coffee maker to remind myself to call the pharmacy in the morning, then went with Danielle into her bedroom to stay with her until she fell asleep.

Twice during the night I found her standing in the freezer, which was oddly reassuring, though not good for her feet. At breakfast, she attacked her waffles so greedily that Bernie practically needed a vacuum to suck out the one she had stuffed in her mouth without chewing or swallowing. I told him that we all needed to practice our Heimlich maneuver technique.

After we walked the dogs and checked on the manatees, I turned on *Sesame Street* so that I could call the pharmacy, anticipating that there might be issues. What I didn't anticipate was the pharmacist telling me the prescription had already been refilled a few days earlier at the store in Lutz, where the foster home was, and that because it was a controlled substance, I could not get it refilled a second time within one month of the first refill. I told the pharmacist there had to be a mistake, but she checked again and said no, it had been picked up on Friday.

I hung up, told Bernie what the pharmacist had said, and asked him to call Garet. A minute later, Garet called and told me that the foster home might have been using the medication for other children. Other children? I thought Danielle was supposed to be the only one there. Garet said that their investigation was showing that while Danielle was supposed to be in the foster family's personal home, she quite possibly had been moved after her visit with us to a group home next door that the agency also supervised. Garet believed that the children there might have scratched Danielle. I was nearly shaking. If they had scratched her, what else might they have done to her? She had no way of telling people if anyone did something to her. Maybe that was why she seemed so withdrawn and distant from us. Garet told me she would look into the procedure for getting more medication. She said that she had gotten the photos of the scratches and had made a report to the agency in our county, so that it would be on record that the scratches had occurred before we picked Danielle up and not with us. I hadn't thought of that, but I was glad Garet did.

Or I was glad until that afternoon. We had a quiet morning in Danielle's room. She played with her Slinky, while I went through the clothes in the duffle bag the foster family had sent. It didn't take long. When I was done, I had a bag with clothes for the trash—they weren't even suitable for Goodwill—topped by the Michelin man bathing apparatus. Danielle was definitely going to need new clothes, but I thought that rather than subjecting all of us to shopping trauma, I would go by myself after dinner, and Danielle could swim in the pool with Bernie and Willie.

We had lunch on the deck, then I put *The Little Mermaid* on for her to watch from the sofa, while I caught up on some of Bernie's paperwork from his jobs. I was so engrossed, I didn't know how long the knocking on the side door had been going on, but it sounded pretty urgent by the time I did hear it. People in the neighborhood knew to come up the exterior stairs to the deck, so I expected that it wasn't anyone we knew. I opened the door onto the deck and shouted down, "Hello? Are you looking for someone?"

A policewoman came around the corner but stood outside the fence. She said she was looking for Danielle Crockett. I told her Danielle was inside and asked how I could help her. She told me the police had received a report of abuse from the DCF in our county and that she was there to investigate and confirm it. I assumed she was talking about the scratches, so I told her to come up the stairs and that Danielle was in the living room.

I offered the policewoman a glass of water, but she declined. She was not being very friendly, but I thought maybe that was just the way she had to be in her line of work. Danielle had barely looked up from the movie and her fascination with Ariel, so the police officer walked over to the sofa and sat down beside her. Danielle scooted away to the far end of the sofa, so I came over to make sure she didn't start a tantrum and pointed out the scratches on her face and arms. "Is this what you're investigating?" I asked.

"Yes, ma'am, that's what I'm looking for. Mrs. Morgan, do you have someone you need to call? You'll need to come with me to the police station."

I was confused. "Mrs. Morgan? Police station? What are you talking about? I'm Diane Lierow, and I'm not going to the police station with you! I have to go pick up my son from school in about five minutes."

"Is he the attacker?"

"The attacker? Willie? No! He's my son! And Danielle came this way!"

The police officer looked skeptical. "You can pick your son up, Mrs. Morgan but I will need to come with you."

"I'm not Mrs. Morgan. I'm Diane Lierow. I don't know why you want to take me to the police station when the abuse happened in the Morgan foster home in Tampa. You don't have your facts straight, lady."

About that time, Danielle started rocking and moaning. I could feel a tantrum coming on and was tempted to let her go for it. Maybe that would drive this misinformed policewoman away. Instead, I picked Danielle up and told the officer I needed to call my husband.

"Is that Mr. Morgan?"

"No! My husband is Bernie Lierow. I'm Diane Lierow, and we picked Danielle up yesterday from Mr. Morgan in Tampa. She is here on an emergency placement. Here's my driver's license."

The policewoman took it from me and examined it while I called Bernie and got his voice mail. "Bernie! You have to come home right now! And call Garet right away! A police officer is here and she thinks I'm Mrs, Morgan and she wants to arrest me! I have to pick up Willie from school. Please get home now!"

Poor Bernie. I was sure he would think I had finally gone off the deep end.

I told the lady I was going to change Danielle's diaper and then I was going to pick my son up from school, and she could wait outside for Bernie to come home. She eyed me suspiciously. I'm not sure whether it was because I was changing the diaper of a child way past diaper stage or she thought I would try to escape out a back window. I invited her to come to the bathroom with me, but she said she would wait in her patrol car, which I discovered was parked in our driveway. Great. That would definitely give the neighborhood something to talk about tonight on the evening walk.

Willie was the last child left at the school when I got there, and he was none too happy about it. I explained what had happened, and we both laughed about the policewoman asking if he was the attacker. If there was any child less likely to be an "attacker" than Willie Lierow, his name would be Ghandi. Ridiculous. At the same time, I was still shaken up by the incident and by how quickly things could have gone very bad. We were already on pins and needles about the possibility that Danielle would be sent back to Tampa. The last thing I needed was the police department here accusing me of abuse. I knew the policewoman would have to make a report of the call, and I didn't want the word *abuse* to be included anywhere near my name. Who knows whether somewhere down the road, as we were moving closer to adoption, this police report might come up and cause more problems?

When we got home, the patrol car was still there, but Bernie's car was, too. Upstairs, he and the policewoman were sitting in the living room like old friends. Darned if she hadn't accepted a soda from Bernie. I scowled at both of them. "Mrs. Lierow, I want to apologize for what happened. I have spoken to Mr. Lierow and Ms. White, and it was all a terrible mix-up. I am so sorry. Is this William?"

The "attacker"? I'm sure that by looking at him, she realized the absurdity of the label. Willie very politely went over to her, shook her hand, and said, "Nice to meet you, ma'am."

She got up to leave, and I was very happy to walk her to the door. While we were chit-chatting, Danielle had slipped over to the refrigerator, opened the double doors, pulled open the bottom drawer, and was standing in the freezer staring into the fridge.

"Danielle!" Bernie, Willie, and I all shouted it at the same time. She turned to look at us with an expression that said, "What? What's the problem?" The policewoman looked confused, but when we all started laughing, she did, too.

"Happens all the time," said Bernie. "No big deal. You should see her with a bag of French fries!"

The officer wished us the best of luck with the adoption procedure and gave Bernie her card. "If you need anything, please let me know. She's a beautiful little girl, and Willie, you're going to make a great big brother."

That ended well. I hoped that it was a sign that things were going to get better.

Unfortunately, things got a bit worse. Because we couldn't get the refill and we didn't have the authority to obtain a new prescription for Danielle, there was no choice but to take her off her medication. I got online to read about weaning people off those particular drugs, and there was some helpful information, but Danielle was going to have to go cold turkey.

The first several days were rough, on her and on us. She screamed constantly. We assumed that she was getting headaches or maybe even migraines from withdrawal. I couldn't legally even give her a single ibuprofen, so I just made the house as dark and quiet as I could and kept her out of the sun. We went out in the evening to walk the dogs, but otherwise, I just tried to let her rest as much as she was able. We needed to keep her as hydrated as possible, but she was also nauseated and would throw up most of what we gave her. Bernie and I hated seeing Danielle that way and had no way to explain to her what was happening. Willie was so upset and worried about her that he slept on the sofa upstairs those first few nights, so that he could get to her quickly if she came out of her room. This was a big help to us. Danielle was waking up every couple of hours, sometimes to pace the house, other times to study the contents of the refrigerator. She never took anything out to eat, and she never tried to open an outside door. We had installed an alarm on all of the outside doors just in case, but she never did try to go out. Maybe she had been conditioned not to in Michelle Crockett's house or in the foster home. Or maybe, just maybe, everything she needed and wanted was inside our house, and she had no desire to leave.

One week after Danielle came home with us, she got up only once in the night, and I heard Willie walk her back to bed. I woke up at six, thinking that something was wrong because it was so quiet. Tiptoeing down the hallway to her room, I nearly tripped over Willie, who was curled up in a quilt on the floor outside her door. Peeking into her room, I saw her lying on her side on the lower mattress, holding Lullaby Gloworm. My heart filled with love for him and his protectiveness for Danielle, and I carefully picked him up and carried him out to the sofa. He barely stirred.

It had been a horrible week: the phone call from Garet, the hurried drive to Tampa, the long wait in the Winn-Dixie parking lot, the scratches, Danielle's distance from us, my near arrest, and her painful withdrawal from medication.

But I felt that the experience had pulled us closer together. We had gotten through it as a family.

I went out to the kitchen to make coffee. The sun was coming up over the canal. It was going to be another beautiful day.

18

T.J. Bearytales

We did not yet have the hard copy of our foster license, but we did have three different social workers, so I assumed we were legitimate and that gave me a little peace of mind. There was one social worker from Florida Baptist Children's Home, where we had started the adoption process, which now seemed like a million years ago; there was Garet from Hillsborough County; and there was one from Lutheran Family Services, the agency responsible for overseeing children in foster care in our county. Florida Baptist is the adoptive or foster family's advocate; Lutheran is the child's advocate. Every child in the system is supposed to be seen once a month by the various agencies responsible for him or her, but it's a system set up to fail. The woman from Lutheran had seventy kids in her caseload. This meant that in one month of weekdays, she would need to see more than three kids a day. If the kids were in school and possibly had after-school activities, that left a very small window of opportunity for her to check on those children.

She told us that if she didn't see Danielle for a couple of months, not to worry. I didn't worry about Danielle. I worried about the children who were not in healthy, stable, caring environments. No wonder there was no scarcity of horror stories about children in foster care.

On the other hand, there was a policy that went to the other extreme. As foster parents in Florida, we could not so much as cut Danielle's hair without getting special permission from the court. It was ludicrous, but after all we had been through to have her in our house, we didn't want to do one thing that could jeopardize this tenuous arrangement. Unfortunately, she still rocked in her bed at night, and as her hair got longer, the morning tangles and knots got worse and worse. I began gathering her hair into a ponytail at the top of her head before putting her to bed, and that helped some, although she looked a bit like Pebbles Flintstone.

Foster parents can get whatever medical treatment is necessary for the children under their care, but dental care was another story. Danielle had never been to a dentist when we got her. In order for her to have a checkup and get her teeth cleaned, we needed to get clearance from the DCS. We knew a dentist in one of the foster parent classes that we had taken, and we asked him whether he could look into her mouth without touching it. He did the best he could under the circumstances and told us there were no obvious signs of decay. I could have said as much from my two years—minus two weeks—in dental hygienist classes.

School was out for the summer, and with so much free time stretching before us, I saw it as an opportunity to create our own life curriculum. We had a girl who was nearly nine years old, with a developmental age of a two-year-old in some critical areas: toilet-training, drinking, and self-feeding. That was ground zero; anything else would be a bonus.

Because Danielle was no longer on medication, her tongue didn't hang out of her mouth, and the drooling had stopped. Aesthetically, that was a big plus. She didn't seem any more hyper than when she was on medication, which had been one concern for us. In reality, she was more alert, and that vacant glaze she had often had in her eyes appeared less frequently. When she did get it, I knew it wasn't from the medication but was probably a coping mechanism she had learned in her previous homes. By the time school started in two and a half months, I hoped that we could master at least one of those toddler development markers, if not all of them.

The first thing Danielle went for when she came to the kitchen every morning was her sippy cup filled with fresh-squeezed orange juice, which I left on the counter for her in case I was in another room. The medication she had been on had given her dry mouth, and she had always been thirsty, which is why her diapers were always soaked. Although she was off the medication, drinking lots of fluids had become habit for her. I thought this would be helpful in transitioning her to a regular cup.

What I foolishly didn't anticipate was that she would treat a regular cup like a sippy cup. Nor did it occur to me to put only a very small amount in the cup. The first time she stood in the kitchen with a real cup, she lifted it to her mouth and turned it upside down, and the entire contents sloshed down her chin and her shirt and onto the floor, where the dogs quickly assembled to lap up some good Florida OJ. This was going to be an education for all of us.

Danielle began to cry, and I wasn't sure whether it was because she was afraid she had done something wrong, because her pajamas were wet, or because the dogs were drinking her juice. I apologized to her, assuring her that mom had made a silly mistake and that I would get her more juice as soon as we got her cleaned up.

Back in the kitchen, I poured a very small amount of juice into the cup and added a straw. When eating at McDonald's, Willie had sometimes shared his milk carton with her, so she was familiar with a straw and the concept.

I held the cup on the table, and she dipped her head to the straw, getting a mouthful of juice. Apparently delighted at the results, she laughed before swallowing, and the juice ran down her chin again. I wiped it off, told her what a smart girl she was, and poured a little bit more in her cup. It took about fifteen minutes, but she eventually drank her eight ounces of juice. Next on the agenda—fun with forks!

Since the first time we had met Danielle at school, we'd had to feed her or serve her finger foods like cut-up fruit, grapes, cubes of cheese, and crackers. Finger foods presented their own challenge because she had no self-regulating button. Similar to her gluttonous approach to French fries, she would just keep stuffing food into her mouth until she went into lock jaw or gagged and got sick. I would cut up a sandwich or a pizza into bite-size pieces at lunch, but I could put only one or two pieces on her plate at a time or she would put all of them in her mouth at once.

Dinner was the most time-consuming meal because Danielle had to be fed every bite. Bernie almost always took on that job because she had been with me all day. He knew from experience, having been Dad and Mom for many years when his boys were growing up, that by five o'clock—the universal witching hour for mothers and children—I needed a break.

Because Danielle loved waffles so much, it made sense to incorporate one into our first lesson in Utensils 101. Willie was up and available to act as her mentor. I cut up one waffle and put it on his plate. "Willie, show Danielle how to use a fork. Danielle, watch Willie with his fork." To his credit, Willie did not roll his eyes at me, although he did get a little bit theatrical with the task. I cut a couple of squares of another waffle for her plate and put a fork in Danielle's hand. She dropped the fork on the table. I tried again. She dropped it on the floor. The third time, I put my hand over hers to hold the fork in place

"Now, Danielle, watch what Willie does with his waffle. See how he puts the bite of waffle on his fork and then puts it in his mouth? Mom knows you can do that, too."

Danielle's eyes were following Willie's hands as he speared a bite of waffle and brought it to his mouth. He had taken about three bites when she couldn't stand it anymore. Her left hand darted across the table. She snatched about three pieces of waffle from his plate and stuffed them in her mouth. She was fast! I shot Willie a look when he started to laugh and then put my fingers in her mouth to pull out the purloined waffle.

"Danielle, we don't take other people's food. If you want to eat, you have to eat from your own plate. Let's try the fork."

I guided her hand to the plate, the fork to the waffle, the forked-waffle to her mouth. "Good job, Danielle! That's the way!" We did it again. Again. Again. Danielle had a voracious appetite. She could and would eat more than anyone else in the house. As long as food was in front of her, she would consume it. Two waffles in, I thought I'd see if she would use the fork on her own.

I put the fork in her hand, removed my hand, and waited. She dropped the fork, grabbed a piece of waffle with her hand, and started to bring it to her mouth. I gently but firmly stopped her, pried the piece out of her hand, put it back on her plate, picked up the fork, and guided it to her mouth.

By the time she finished three waffles, her face was sticky with syrup, and I could have used a nap. Instead, we moved to the next class. Toilet training.

As far as I could remember, it had taken anywhere from a couple of weeks to a couple of months for Paul, Steven, and Willie to transition from diapers through pull-ups to consistent use of the toilet during the day. I was always prepared for accidents in that first year, and I accepted that staying dry through the night was more of a challenge for children, especially for heavy sleepers. I had to wake one of my boys up every three hours or so during the night to take him to the bathroom well past toddlerhood, or he'd wake up in a wet bed every morning.

I was prepared to be in it for the long haul with Danielle, although I figured that if we did total immersion, she might just get so sick of being in the bathroom that she would take the alternative—and the M&M's, which I had used with the boys as a reward for doing something on the toilet, much as I had used little doggie treats to house-train Cece, Bebe, and Inky.

But nothing could pry a pee out of Danielle if she wasn't in the mood. We would sit and sit, I would read her two or three books, then read them again. Not even a tinkle. Until I would say, "Okay, I give up," then she would stand and go all over herself and the floor. I believed that she knew what I wanted her to do, and that peeing on the floor was a statement of some kind from her. An annoying statement, to be sure, but any sign that she was taking deliberate action was a good sign. Maybe she was testing me. Whatever it was, I was determined to outlast her, and in the meantime, I put a towel on the floor beside the toilet to absorb her "statement."

Bowel movements were another issue altogether. Long before we even knew Danielle existed or that we would try to adopt, Bernie saw a commercial on television for a toy called T.J. Bearytales. It was an animated electronic teddy bear that came with a storybook and a cartridge, aimed at three- to five-year-olds, which explains why Bernie loved it so much. He became obsessed with T.J. Bearytales, calling me to the television each time the goofy ad came on. I kept pointing out that Willie was well past the T.J. Bearytales stage, but Bernie thought it would be perfect for our future grandchildren.

We generally try to avoid Target. There is something very manipulative about that store. We could go in for a sale it was having on storage bins, walk out with patio furniture, an electric frying pan, and beach towels—and forget the storage bins. One afternoon we ventured in for a new inflatable raft for the pool—blinders firmly affixed to the sides of our eyes—when Bernie gasped. "T.J. Bearytales!"

There, right in our path, was a huge display of T.J. Bearytales. One was powered up and ready to read. Fuzzy arms waving, lit eyes blinking, story cartridge in place in his back, T.J. was telling the compelling tale of his Beary First Day of School. I thought it was kind of creepy, but Bernie could not be dissuaded. Thirty minutes later, we walked out of Target with T.J. Bearytales—and didn't realize we had forgotten the raft until we got home.

Within a week, I had put T.J. away and forgotten about him. I thought Bernie had, too.

One evening, as both of us sat in the bathroom with Danielle reading her a book and hoping for a bowel movement or a miracle, whichever came first, the proverbial lightbulb went off over Bernie's head. "T.J. Bearytales! Where is he?" "In the storage closet downstairs, under the crib." Bernie darted out the door and five minutes later was back, proudly carrying a slightly dusty T.J. He set the bear on the edge of the tub and pushed the button, and T.J's mechanical but very enthusiastic voice began the story of his Bearific trip to outer space. Bernie held the book up so that Danielle could see the pictures, but she couldn't take her eyes off T.J. She was hypnotized. She didn't do anything on the toilet that night—except sit quietly while T.J. told stories.

A couple of days later, I went to her room to look for her. I didn't see her, but I could hear her from behind the partially closed door of her closet. I slowly opened it, and she was squatting, having a bowel movement in her diaper. It occurred to me that maybe she wanted more privacy for this particular function.

The next day, I put Danielle in the bathroom alone with T.J., turned him on to loop the story, and left her there for about ten minutes. When I got back, she was still engrossed in the Bearytale, but she had also had a bowel movement in the toilet. Success! I was so excited, I called Bernie on his cell phone. I can only imagine what the guys he was working with thought when he exclaimed, "She pooped? In the potty? With the poopie bear?" From then on,

T.J. was known as Poopie Bear, and that silly toy turned out to be a godsend. Training Danielle to urinate on the toilet was not meeting with the same degree of success, and I told Bernie to be on the lookout for a Pee Pee Puppy.

Nearly one month from the time Danielle came to live with us, we received an 8×10 envelope from Children's Network of Southwest Florida. Things like that always made me nervous, and I held it up to the light, trying to determine the contents. I could see an official seal, and, practically holding my breath, I tore it open. "Dear Mr. and Mrs. Lierow: Enclosed is your foster license to provide foster care service for children placed in your care. The number of children you may accept is specified on the license as 'capacity.'"

I stared at our "Certificate of License" issued on May 29, 2007, although it hadn't been mailed out until June 21. I had been so worried that something would happen; that without the official certificate, Danielle could have been taken from us. Bernie kept telling me not to worry, but I could tell he was anxious about it as well. Every step of the way with Danielle had been such a nail biter. I knew we wouldn't feel totally secure until the adoption was finalized. But this was helpful in making us feel legitimate.

The license had to be posted in a prominent location, although I couldn't imagine why. It wasn't as if birth parents had to post their children's birth certificates in a prominent place.

I wanted to surprise Bernie, so I tacked the certificate on the outside of the door that he always used when he came home from work. I put it exactly at his eye level so he couldn't miss it. And he didn't. Two minutes after I heard his truck pull into the drive and him clumping up the exterior staircase in his clunky work boots, I heard, "Woo hoo!" and I knew he had found it. He flew in the door with the license clutched in his hands. "Diane! We got our license! Did you see it?"

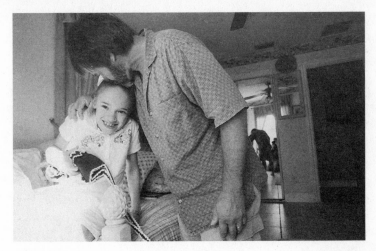

A hug from Dad.

I looked sideways at him. "Who do you think put it up there, Bernie?" He grabbed me in a big hug, then Willie, and finally Danielle, whom he picked up and twirled around and around in circles. She had no idea what we were so happy about, but she loved when Daddy spun her around in his arms, just as if she was flying.

We went out to dinner to celebrate, and to make things simple, we ordered chicken fingers and French fries for Danielle. No lessons tonight. As the waitress picked up our menus, she remarked what beautiful children we had. I couldn't agree with her more.

19

Pedal, Pedal, Pedal!

Willie, Danielle, and I had our summer routine down pat. In the mornings after breakfast and walking the dogs and before it got too hot, we went to the beach. It was close enough to walk—just across the road from the entrance to Laguna Shores—but with all of the buckets, the shovels, Danielle's life jacket, the ball, the towels, a chair for me, sunscreen, and a cooler with drinks and fruit, it was easier to drive.

All along the main road on Estero Island, there were pockets of beach access parking. Then it was only a short walk across a boardwalk to the beach. Danielle could carry her towel or a small bag, Willie and I hauled the rest. She wasn't interested in anything except getting in the water, and we took frequent breaks to gather seashells in baggies I brought. I pointed out Danielle's footprints to her when she used her flat feet, which we were encouraging her to do on a consistent basis. Dorothy wanted to know why we just didn't get her a pair of toe shoes and turn her into a ballerina.

"She has the shape for it," Dorothy said. "Long and lean. She's not clumsy. She likes to spin and jump. And she already has *en pointe* mastered. She could be a prodigy, for all you know!"

Willie tried to teach Danielle to dig with a shovel but without success. She did like it when I helped her fill a bucket with water, then pour it into the hole Willie had excavated in the sand. She had come a long way since the first day we brought her to the beach, when she had cried at the feel of the sand on her feet. Now she rolled in it, and getting the sand out of her hair and every orifice was a challenge.

Around eleven we'd pack everything up, rinse off with the hose at the edge of the parking lot, and go back to the house for lunch and to get out of Florida's brutal midday sun.

Danielle was getting better with the cup. She graduated from a straw to picking her cup up as Willie did and drinking the small amounts I put in for her, then banging the cup on the table when she wanted more. If I told her to use words, she responded by banging the cup again. At least she knew what she wanted, but I was torn between rewarding her for something I felt that she could improve on and expecting too much too soon. Spoons and forks were still a stumbling block, although we practiced every day. I got her a little toy kitchen set with plastic plates, bowls, cups, and utensils, and Willie often staged "pretend" meals on the deck or the floor of Danielle's room.

Willie loved art and could amuse himself for hours with the big box full of art supplies I collected for him: paints, brushes, crayons, markers, glue, tape, wallpaper, tile and carpet samples, clay, pipe cleaners, construction paper, cardboard, felt scraps, and glitter. Art projects took place on the deck as well, so I could watch the kids outside the kitchen window. Danielle liked to "help," and Willie was very patient, putting paint on a brush for her and guiding her hand to whatever surface she used. She put everything in her mouth, so he kept her away from the clay and the glue. Finger paints were her favorite—the nontoxic kind—and she managed to get as much on the paper as she did on the table. I studied her Rorschach creations carefully to see if I could glean any hidden meanings or subconscious messages from her, but as Bernie pointed out, "Sometimes a smear is just a smear, Diane."

Danielle loved the pool. We told her when she first came to live with us that she must never go into the pool without one of us with her, and she never did. She waited until Bernie or I asked, "Danielle, do you want to swim in the pool?" and her entire body would react the way a dog does when you hold up a leash.

One Sunday afternoon while I was in the kitchen making brownies to take to the church supper that night, Bernie spoke the magic words. I got Danielle into her suit and sent her downstairs. Bernie and Willie were already in the pool. Five minutes later, I heard them shouting, "Diane! Mom!" and I dashed down the stairs and out the door. Both of them were in the water, but where was Danielle? Her life jacket was on a lounge chair. They seemed awfully calm to be witnessing a drowning. In fact, Bernie was positively beaming.

Suddenly, Danielle's head popped up. She blinked her eyes, took a breath, and went under again. I could see her lithe body traverse the bottom of the pool until she got to the ladder, climbed up and out, walked to the edge, and jumped back in. She was remarkably graceful. She was as comfortable in the water as an Olympic swimmer.

I gave Bernie the fish eye. "Did you let her jump in the pool without her life jacket?" He laughed. "There was no time to 'let' her do anything, Diane. She came out the door, walked straight to the edge of the pool, and jumped in. She was on a mission." "He's right, Mom! There wasn't anything we could do!"

Danielle was so happy, plunging underwater to the bottom, then back up to the surface, where she would roll and splash, then skim across the surface to the other side. She didn't so much swim as glide, like a seal or a mermaid. Our own Ariel. No wonder she became so engrossed in *The Little Mermaid* when I played it for her.

I knew darn well Danielle had never had a swimming lesson. Until she left her mother's home, she had rarely been in a bathtub, much less a pool. She had never been to the beach, despite living in Florida most of her life. The foster parents had put her in that ridiculous contraption that prevented her from putting her head underwater, which is what she seemed to like the most. How had she learned to hold her breath? To open her eyes underwater? To move so effortlessly? To plunge into the unknown so fearlessly?

Dorothy came by one afternoon to drop off some clothes that her granddaughters had long ago out grown. I had told her that Danielle was no longer using the life jacket, and I could tell she was a little concerned. Dorothy was probably delivering the clothes as an excuse to see for herself. Willie and Danielle were in the pool. After Dorothy spent a few moments watching Danielle, she turned to me. "It's unbelievable. It's like the water is the one place she is totally free." Dorothy was right. In the water, it didn't matter that Danielle couldn't read or speak or use a fork. Her entire body was embraced by the water, and no one could harm her. Instinctively, she went back to the womb, the last place she had been safe before she was delivered to her mother. What a cruel trick that had been! I vowed to myself that no matter what, no matter where we lived, we would always have a pool for Danielle.

She also loved jumping. She jumped on the sofa, she jumped on the chairs, she jumped on the beds. This was not an approved activity in our house, and Danielle understood that pretty quickly. If she did slip and her jumping needs got the best of her, the minute she saw Bernie or me, she stopped. She knew what she was allowed to do and what she wasn't, which was very encouraging to us.

Dorothy allowed Danielle to jump on one bed in her house, and that was Amber's bed. It didn't have much spring left, but it suited an old fat dog and an eight-year-old girl with a jumping obsession just fine. The first thing Danielle did when we dropped by Dorothy and Paul's was run to the bed, climb up, and start springing up and down like a pogo stick. She was the only human Dorothy spoiled worse than she did her dog. I told Dorothy that if we ever moved, she would have to sell me that bed.

Instead, Bernie came home one evening with a mini-trampoline, less than a foot off the ground and about four feet across. It was just big enough for one person, and that one person knew it was for her right away. Willie demonstrated and then just got out of Danielle's way. I was afraid she was going to go right through the ceiling, but the closest she got—even with her most invigorated attempts—left a good foot of clearance. Eventually, as those long legs of hers continued to grow, the trampoline would have to be moved outside.

The mini-trampoline the Lierows bought Danielle so that she would stop jumping on furniture.

For now, she enjoyed sitting on it as much as jumping on it, and that became her perch for the hour each afternoon when I let her and Willie watch television. Danielle is incredibly limber and flexible and can practically turn herself inside out. She also has excellent posture, which was surprising to us, considering that she spent so much of her life curled up on a mattress in a fetal position. Maybe Dorothy was right. Danielle did have the form of a ballerina, though it was hard to imagine a ballerina in pull-up diapers saying woo-woo-woo.

When Bernie came home from work, he liked to play with the kids in the yard, throwing and kicking a ball, playing chase and hide and seek. He staged races and tried to teach Danielle how to do a somersault.

What he and Willie really wanted, though, was for Danielle to learn to ride a bike. Willie often rode his two-wheeler while we walked the dogs in the evening, and he would have loved for Danielle to ride with him.

So, we all went to Wal-Mart to peruse its bikes and see what Danielle took to before we invested in anything. At first, she took to nothing. She cried and yelled and did her best to make other shoppers think we were torturing her.

Bernie got a tricycle and put it at the end of the aisle, away from the other bikes, and got Danielle to sit on it by distracting her with her Slinky. He slowly pushed her back and forth on it, only a couple inches in each direction because her feet were planted firmly on the floor as if to say, "I'm not going anywhere!" She seemed fine with that, so while I took her over to look at talking toys, Bernie found the biggest tricycle in the store, bought it, and put it in the rear cargo container of the truck.

The official riding lessons began in our driveway, with Danielle on her tricycle and Willie on his big boy bike, demonstrating the concept of pedaling. "See, Danielle, you put a foot on each pedal, and when you push down with one, the other one comes up and then it moves the bike. Then you push down again on the pedal. You can do it!"

Bernie sat Danielle on the tricycle and put one foot on each pedal. She looked like one of those Shriner Circus clowns who rides the tricycles and the Big Wheels in parades and makes you laugh just because he looks so ridiculous on a tricycle. Danielle's legs were so long that when Bernie guided her foot to push down on one pedal, the knee coming up banged into the handlebars. If he got her knee past the handlebars, then it hit her in the chin.

After a week or so, she was able to go forward and backward in the driveway with encouragement from Willie, but that was not exactly what he had in mind as a riding partner.

Bill and Doris and some friends of theirs from the street over were watching one evening, and the man mentioned that they had a small two-wheeler with training wheels in their garage that they kept for their granddaughters. The girls had moved away, and we were welcome to try it. A few minutes later he came back with an adorable pink bike with plastic streamers from the handlebars. Danielle must have been tired of being attacked by her own knees because when she saw it, she hoisted herself up onto the seat while Bernie held the bike so that she didn't topple over.

They went out into the street, and while Willie reviewed the fundamentals, Bernie placed Danielle's feet on the pedals. Then, just as I had done for Paul and Steven, as Bernie had done for Shawn and Ryan, as we had both done for Willie, as parents have done for their children probably since the invention of the wheel, Bernie set off down the road with his little girl on her first bike. His hand on her back giving her the slightest push, he trotted along beside her, urging, "Pedal, pedal, pedal!" as Willie coasted behind them. I ran to catch up as they went down the street, passing neighbors in their yards who cheered Danielle on as if she were wearing the yellow shirt in the Tour de France.

At the corner, we all turned around to go back to our driveway, and as we passed our neighbors again, they all shouted out to her, "Pedal, Danielle, pedal!" With her father at her side and her brother with her back, she seemed to float. The only motion was her feet pushing the pedals up and down, round and round.

20

Dani

Summer vacation was more than halfway over when Garet called with the news we had been waiting to hear: the Court of Appeals had affirmed the Termination of Parental Rights. The appellate court saw no grounds for the TPR to be overturned, and it was upheld. Finally, someone and something was making sense. Almost exactly two years to the day since Danielle was rescued from her mother's house, she was officially and legally available for adoption.

We had hoped so much that the adoption would go through before her ninth birthday on September 21, but, ironically, there was one more thing standing in the way—the missing birth certificate.

An adoption could not be completed without one. Once again, it was Michelle Crockett acting as a human road block. She told the DCF that she had no birth certificate for Danielle, that maybe it had been lost in the fire, and she never got another one. She told the DCF she couldn't remember exactly where in Nevada Danielle had been born, maybe Las Vegas. Bernie and I were sure she was lying. Even if she couldn't remember the name of the hospital, she could surely remember the town, especially if it was Las Vegas, as she had previously said many times. But she played ignorant, and the DCF was forced to send out dozens of birth certificate requests to Nevada.

Another month—and Danielle's ninth birthday—passed, and our frustration mounted again. Every time I got a note from school or something in the mail referencing Danielle Crockett, I became irritated. She was Crockett in name only; in every other way, she was a Lierow. We knew that in our hearts. We saw it in her every day as she eased into our family and was becoming the person she had never had the freedom or security to be.

Danielle playing with the Easy Bake oven that she got for her birthday.

Finally, in mid-October, Garet received the birth certificate for Danielle Ann Crockett and faxed us a copy. As it turned out, Danielle had been born at Sunrise Hospital and Medical Center, in Las Vegas, Clark County, Nevada, at 5:27 p.m. on September 21, 1998. The attending physician was Dr. Richard Litt; the mother, Michelle Sara Crockett. The space for the father's name was blank.

Garet told us that a court date for the adoption hearing had been set for October 29, a Monday, and asked whether that was okay with us. If the hearing had been set for Christmas Day, it would have been okay for us, but as it turned out, there was no school that day so we would all be able to go. The hearing would take place in Tampa, because that was where Danielle had been taken into custody. All that we had to do was show up.

I wanted to make a good impression on the judge, so we all dressed in our Sunday clothes. It was hard for me to let go of that flutter of nerves knowing that at any moment Danielle could be taken from us or someone might change his or her mind, and we'd be back in limbo again or worse.

We were set to appear at 2:45 p.m. before Judge Katherine Essrig in the George R. Edgecomb Courthouse. Garet said she would meet us in the building's lobby and suggested we get there about thirty minutes early.

We were all so glad to see Garet, who had been in the hospital for brain surgery between the time we last saw her and that day. I told Bernie it was probably his fault, as much as he had called her during the last year, and I was only half-kidding. Garet was not required to be at the hearing, but as close as we had all become, as much as she had advocated for Danielle, and as personal as this case was for her, she said she wouldn't have missed it for anything.

Garet had brought Danielle a little goodie bag with crayons, coloring books, and little things to occupy her in the very small room where we had to wait, and it worked for a while. But when

Danielle with Garet White.

Danielle got up from the cushioned chair she had been sitting in, she had wet through her pull-ups. I took her to the restroom to put on another pair of pull-ups and dry her clothes as best I could with paper towels and the hand-blower on the wall. I was relieved no one else came in while we were there, and hoped that this one would last at least through the court proceedings.

When we got back, Willie was nearly bouncing off the walls from the two cans of soda he had consumed while we were waiting, Danielle was edging toward a hissy fit, Bernie was cranky because he was hungry, and I had a raging headache and terrible cramps. Not exactly the happy, feel-good moment I had dreamed about.

Mercifully, the lawyer assigned to our case found us, introduced herself, and led us to the courtroom. Despite my best intentions that morning, I'm sure we looked like a motley crew.

We stood before the judge, and she announced that all of the papers were in order and asked us if we wanted to be the parents of Danielle Ann Crockett. We said yes. Then, in most cases, the judge asks the child, "Do you want Diane and Bernie Lierow to be your parents?" It's kind of like that moment in a wedding ceremony when the preacher says, "If anyone has just cause for this ceremony not to take place, speak now or forever hold your peace." I can't imagine that anyone has ever taken a preacher up on that invitation, although I briefly wondered whether a child about to be adopted had ever had a last-minute change of mind and said, "No, as a matter of fact, I don't want these people to be my parents."

Danielle couldn't speak for herself, so Garet spoke for her. "Yes, the Lierows are wonderful people. They have bonded with Danielle since the moment they met. We want very much for them to be her parents."

The judge then said, "I'm granting the adoption. Danielle Ann Lierow is now your daughter." There was probably a lot more legal language than that, but "Danielle Ann Lierow is now your daughter" was the only sentence Bernie and I heard. The words we had been waiting for almost since the first day we met Danielle.

After all that we had been through, after all that Danielle had been through, it took all of five minutes for Danielle Ann Crockett to become Danielle Ann Lierow. When we left the courtroom, we took photos with Garet and with complete strangers who had heard about the case and wanted their pictures made with our family. It was a little bit weird to be treated as if we were celebrities just because we did something we were called to do.

As soon as we got the Final Judgment of Adoption signed by the judge and sealed by the State of Florida, we were done. They would send a copy to Nevada to have a new birth certificate issued, and it would be mailed to our house. We would not have to go back to court. We walked with Garet to the garage, hugged one another all around, and got in the car. We just wanted to be out of there and to put Tampa in our rearview mirror, hopefully for good.

After we stopped and ate at the Venice McDonald's, Danielle and Willie both fell asleep in the backseat, slumped toward the middle, their heads resting on the pile of stuffed animals we kept in the car for Danielle. Back on Tarpon Road, we carried the kids into the house, sent Willie to brush his teeth and put on his pajamas, and took Danielle to change her diaper and put her nightgown on. I didn't have the energy to pull out the trundle, so Bernie just laid Danielle on the upper mattress and covered her with the Hello Kitty comforter. He turned out the light, switched on the nightlight, kissed the top of Danielle's head, and pulled the door partly shut.

We crawled into bed, utterly exhausted from the ordeal of that long day. Bernie asked me how I felt. "I have a pounding headache and brutal cramps. You?" He laughed. "I meant do you feel any different?" "No, not really. You?" "Nope."

When I went to Danielle's bedroom to wake her the next morning, I was relieved to see that she had not rocked herself off and fallen to the floor but was still on the bed. Other than that, the first morning that Danielle woke up as a Lierow was just like every other day—she got out of the pull-up, sat on the toilet, ate, dressed, threw a tantrum while her hair was brushed, got in the car, and went to school.

After school and a snack, Willie always did his homework in the kitchen so I could make sure he stayed focused and could give him help if he needed it. Danielle didn't have "homework" like Willie's, but if I knew she was working on the letter *c* or the number 3, we did activities to reinforce her lessons. Cup, cookie, cracker. One cup, two cookies, three crackers. Pretty rudimentary stuff, and how responsive she was depended on her mood or the carrot I dangled in front of her. "Danielle, if you show me two cookies, you can eat one cookie. " Willie reached out his hand to grab the other cookie.

"William Christian Lierow, you've already had your cookie allotment. You don't need any more sugar. Now put that cookie back, and put your eyes back on that spelling list. Your sister doesn't need your help right now."

"Mom, why do you call me by my full name when you're mad at me?"

"Because it gets your attention. You know I mean business when I say, 'William Christian Lierow,' right?"

"I guess. How long have you and Dad been calling me Willie?"

"Pretty much since you were born. Your given name is William, but when you were a baby, you looked like a Willie. We could have called you Bill or Billy, but you've always been a Willie. Your dad's given name in Bernd, which is the German form of Bernard. But he's always been Bernie."

"What is your full name?"

"Diane Lee Lierow. My maiden name was Spenser, so when Grandma wanted to get my attention, she would say, 'Diane Lee Spenser!' And I knew to snap to."

"What is Danielle's full name?"

"Danielle Ann Lierow."

"Why doesn't she have a shorter name?" Willie was on one of his question binges and was looking for any reason not to do his spelling, but it was an interesting train of thought. Danielle was eyeing the second cookie, trying to figure out if she could get it without my noticing. Fat chance of that. I am the queen of 360-degree vision.

"I mean, if her given name is Danielle and you always call her Danielle, how will she know when you mean business?"

I had to admit, he had a point. I hadn't really thought about it. As much as Bernie and I would have liked to wipe the slate clean, erase every single thing from her life with Michelle Crockett, we just couldn't change her name. She didn't know her father, she didn't know where she was born, she probably had never really known where she lived because she had been kept in one room all her life, but she did know her name. Still, a revision might not be a bad thing. It could be something we gave her. If Bernie and I were giving her "Lierow," maybe this could be Willie's contribution to her becoming a fully invested member of our patchwork family.

"Well, what would you suggest, William Christian Lierow?" He looked at me warily, not sure if I was getting annoyed at him or kidding with him. I smiled and waited. I could almost see the little wheels in his head turning.

"Does Danny sound too much like a boy's name?" he asked.

"I don't know. Danny is a boy's name, but Danielle is the feminine version of Daniel, so I guess it's one of those names that can go both ways. Like Samuel and Samantha can be Sam or Sammy. Or Jack and Jacqueline; she can be Jack or Jackie. So I guess Danielle could be a Danny. How would you spell it?"

William looked puzzled. "I don't know. How is a boy Danny spelled?"

"D-A-N-N-Y."

"I think we should spell it like a girl. How would that be spelled?"

I got out a piece of paper and wrote down "Daniel" and "Danny." Then I wrote "Danielle" and "Danni." Dannie? Dani? I showed them to Willie and asked him which he thought was best.

"Well, I think when it's time for her to learn how to write her name, it would be easier for her to write D-A-N-I."

One minute Willie could be driving me batty with endless questions, and the next he could knock me out with his thoughtfulness. What a great way to look at it! I told him it sounded good to me, but that I'd just like for us to run it by his dad first.

At the dinner table that night, I prompted Willie to bring it up. "Willie, why don't you tell your dad what you were thinking about Danielle's name?" Bernie put his fork down. Willie was a little bit nervous, and, after he took a deep breath, his proposal came out in one sentence.

"You know how I'm a Willie even though I'm William, and you're a Bernie even though you're a Bernd, and I was thinking that Danielle could be a Dani, spelled D-A-N-I, and that way her name will be easier for her to write than 'Danielle' and also when

Mom is mad at her, she can say, 'Danielle Ann Lierow,' like she says, 'William Christian Lierow,' and that way Dani will know that Mom means business and she could be in trouble."

When Bernie looked at me, I winked, our signal for "Okay with me." He turned to Willie and said, "That sounds like a well-thought-out plan, Willie. I like it."

Willie grinned, then turned to Danielle. "What do you think, Dani? Do you want to be called Dani? Do you like that name, Dani?"

Danielle, now Dani, kept eating. Food was still her focus, and what we chose to call her was not her concern.

Halloween was the next day, and thanks to the trip to Tampa, we still didn't have a costume for Dani. Willie had been working with Paul for weeks, planning an interpretation of Captain Jack, and from what I had seen so far, it was going to be pretty outrageous. Dani needed to be equally spectacular. After dinner, we drove to the Disney store at the Fort Myers mall, along with dozens of other families who had waited until the last minute to get a costume. It was madness, and I just wanted to grab an Ariel and be done with it. Bernie was more patient, walking around with Dani and showing her all of the different options. Willie was also scouting, so I stood at the entrance of the store to make sure no one slipped away with our kids, although I'm pretty certain that if anyone took Dani, they'd bring her right back.

"Dad! Mom! Come here! Look at this one!" I followed Willie's voice to the Peter Pan display, where he stood beside a mannequin in a gorgeous burgundy satin tunic, trimmed in black brocade, over aqua satin pants. A black sash went around her waist and a gold-embroidered vest topped the tunic. Dani reached out to touch it and smiled. That was all it took. Bernie bit the hook, and she reeled him in. I gulped when I saw the price tag and hoped that Dani didn't mind being a Pirate Princess for the rest of her lifetime of Halloweens.

The next night, Paul came over to help transform Willie into Captain Jack Sparrow, while I dressed Dani in our bedroom. With all of the time we had spent outdoors that summer, Dani's hair had turned golden blond, and it shimmered against the vest. The colors of the costume complemented her tanned skin, and she looked every inch the beautiful princess. Bernie came in to check our progress, and his mouth dropped open. He stood her in front of the full-length mirror to see herself, and her eyes opened wide. "Dani, look at the pretty princess! Who is that pretty princess? It's Princess Danielle, isn't it? You are such a pretty princess!" As Paul and Willie watched from the door, Dani stepped up to the mirror and kissed her image, as if to say, "Oh yes, I am pretty, aren't I?"

With Princess Danielle in her colorful splendor and Captain Willie Jack in a long wig, black eye liner, a menacing goatee, and a swashbuckler sword, the two made quite an impression as we looped the neighborhood. Everyone wanted to take a photo, and very uncharacteristically, Dani was patient, as if doing her adoring

Willie as Captain Jack and Dani as a Disney princess.

audience a magnanimous favor. She caught on quickly that all she had to do was open her bag after Willie said, "Trick or Treat!" and the nice people at the door would drop in some candy and tell her how pretty she was.

Bernie and I were walking several paces behind them, letting Willie lead the way. Bernie put his arm around my shoulder and pulled me close. "They make a pretty good team, don't they?" I had to agree they did.

The week before Thanksgiving, we got a brown government envelope in the mail from the State of Nevada. I pulled out two sheets of paper. The one on top was very simple: a cover letter from the Nevada Department of Health and Human Services. "Attached is the original copy of the birth certificate for Danielle Ann Lierow. Please store in a secure location with other vital records."

The other sheet of paper was the new birth certificate we had been waiting for. The same time and date of birth, hospital, city, county, state, and physician were listed. The same State of Nevada seal was displayed across the top. But on this version, the child's name was Danielle Ann Lierow, the mother was Diane Lee Lierow, and the father Bernd Lierow.

I had never been to Las Vegas, had never even been in the state of Nevada, and now I seemingly had given birth there. But it could have said Mars, Universe, across the top, for all I cared. I pressed it to my heart, so very relieved. We didn't need a piece of paper to confirm that Dani was our daughter, but for the first time since we had brought her home at Easter, I felt legally secure as her mother. We would not have to be afraid anymore that someone could take her away from us. I showed the document to Bernie that night, then filed it away with the birth certificates for me, Bernie, Shawn, Ryan, Paul, Steven, and Willie. And Dani makes eight.

21

Baby's First Christmas

Dani was tolerating school better—she loved her speech therapist Leslie Goldenberg and was warming up to her primary teacher—but she still had mini-tantrums when she saw the backpacks by the door on Monday mornings. Home was where her heart was, being with her family and the dogs. Toilet training was going well. When Dani wasn't in school, she wore underwear until it was time for bed. Bernie or I reminded her or took her at least once an hour to go to the bathroom. She would pull her own pants down and sit on the toilet until something happened, even if it was just a tiny trickle. I usually handed her some toilet paper; otherwise, she wouldn't use it at all and would drip dry, or she would unwind an entire roll onto the floor.

Dani learned not to swipe things from other people's plates—not that she always resisted the temptation, but she knew it was wrong. We made her use her spoon and fork, which slowed her down and kept her from stuffing more food in her mouth than she

With speech therapist Leslie Goldenberg, whom Dani loved. Obviously.

could chew. I think she finally realized that there would be another opportunity to eat, and she didn't have to hoard.

Though she couldn't play board games with Willie, as he had hoped, Dani and he had fun together, swimming and riding their bikes, with Willie constantly reminding her, "Pedal, Dani, pedal!" He could get her to hold Bebe's leash when we walked the dogs if he held Cece's and walked beside her. The Easy-Bake oven we got Dani for her birthday was a huge hit. Dani wore the apron and stirred; Willie measured and poured. It was amazing how much of the dry mix she could get everywhere but in the bowl. When the timer went off, she knew exactly what it meant—cake!

We got a battery-powered riding jeep for Willie, who spent a good part of one afternoon washing it and tricking out the bright-red body with flags and stickers. It was just big enough for the two of them to squeeze into. Willie drove and Dani rode shotgun and pushed the button for the horn. When Dorothy saw them coming, she hollered, "Here comes Willie, driving Miss Dani!" Dani would have been

Dani on the stairs at the Lierows' house.

In the jeep with Willie.

happy to ride around like that all day, every day. All that she lacked was a tiara, a sash, and the classic beauty queen wave.

I cut back a bit on my hours with my part-time job at a property management company. It brought in a little extra money for things like Building Blocks speech therapy and dinner out a couple of nights a week, but I also needed to be available to take Dani to Building Blocks which was in Naples, about a 30-minute drive from our house. Luckily, my boss was very flexible, and I was able to be home for the kids before and after school. On weekends, we went to arts or music festivals, to outdoor flea markets, and to window shop in old Florida communities near where we lived. I gave Dani some of my old purses to play with, and she loved to carry one while we shopped, just like a big girl.

As a Yankee, I still hadn't adjusted to shorts and balmy weather in the winter, but it was preferable to boots, gloves, and long underwear. Christmas was different, though. I think that wherever you have grown up, you dream of that miraculous white Christmas. It was the only time of the whole year that I missed the north.

To get myself into the spirit, as soon as I put away the Thanksgiving gourds and the turkey platter, I pulled all of our decorations out of storage and turned the house into a combination of Bethlehem and the North Pole. This year I had to be more cautious about the smaller items that might end up in Dani's mouth. When we trimmed the tree, she kept batting at the ornaments, so she and Bernie sat in the daddy chair and watched Willie and me decorate from a safe distance.

Willie had outgrown sitting on Santa's lap with his Christmas list, and I wasn't sure how Dani would handle visiting Santa in a crowded mall. But Grandpa Bill had a Santa costume, and he volunteered to dress up for Dani. I don't think she really understood what was going on, who Santa was, or what he was doing at the Kennys' house, but she gobbled up Doris's Christmas cookies.

It was getting dark early enough that when we walked the dogs after dinner, all of the Christmas lights in the neighborhood were on. Dani loved that, especially the ones that twinkled on and off. She was drawn to the inflatable Santas, elves, and snowmen, just as she had been to Bill's Easter bunny, and she wanted to hug and kiss them all. Bernie, Willie, and I were so excited about Dani's first Christmas, we could hardly stand it. Willie helped me pick out and wrap her presents. He was so patient, showing her how to make a garland out of strips of red and green construction paper and paste.

December was an especially frenetic month in our family, because on top of the normal Christmas frenzy, three of our five boys were December babies—Ryan's birthday was December 15, Willie turned ten on December 16, and Paul was born on December 24.

Paul and his girlfriend Angela came over for his birthday dinner on Christmas Eve, and we had the Lierow family birthday ice cream cake for dessert. After they left, we watched *A Christmas Carol*, the Muppets version, then I read *The Night before Christmas* before putting the kids to bed. Dani was a little restless, but we attributed it to the cake and the cookies, if not visions of sugarplums dancing in her head.

It was our tradition to put all of the family gifts around the tree on Christmas Eve after the kids went to sleep. While I pulled bags and boxes out of closets and from under our bed, Bernie got the bigger presents we had hidden in the trunk of the car or at Bill and Doris's house. There was always something to put together. This year it was two new bikes. Dani had outgrown the one we got from the neighbor in the fall. Willie's was a couple of years old, so we picked one out for him that we thought he might grow into. We parked the bikes on each side of the tree and piled the packages around those.

It wasn't yet dawn on Christmas morning when we heard Dani shrieking, loud and frantic. Both of us leaped out of bed and ran toward the sound, knocking into Willie, who was doing the same. Dani was in the living room. She had stripped off her pajamas and pull-ups. Her hair was every which way, and she was crying, biting her arm, hitting herself in the thighs, and pacing on her toes. She looked terrified. When Bernie approached her, she ran screeching through the kitchen to the dining room. Her eyes were open, but it was almost as if she was sleepwalking. I could see that Willie was scared, and I asked him to go get one of Dani's fuzzy throw blankets from her bed, mostly to get him away from the sight of Dani having a buck-naked meltdown. I poured a cup of juice for her, while Bernie quietly reassured her, letting her know everything was okay and that she was safe. She began to calm down. Willie handed his dad the blanket, and Bernie wrapped Dani up in it and carried her whimpering like a baby back to her room.

She had no way of telling us what had happened or what had frightened her so much. We think she must have had a nightmare that woke her up. Then when she came out of her bedroom to find someone to help her, the living room probably looked so unfamiliar with the bikes, the toys, and the tree that she got completely disoriented and terrified. What compelled her to take her clothes off was a mystery, as many things still were with Dani.

I put her in another pull-up and clean pajamas. While Bernie and Willie stayed with her in her bedroom, playing with her stuffed animals, I went to the kitchen to start coffee and put a pan of cinnamon sweet rolls in the oven. I plugged in the lights on the tree and turned on a CD of Christmas carols. The sun was coming up when the three of them came back into the living room. The smell of cinnamon buns wafted from the kitchen, and the sweet, sad words of "I'll Be Home for Christmas" filled the room. Dani sat cross-legged on the floor beside Willie. Her eyes were still teary from crying, but she gave him a tentative smile when he handed her a package wrapped in Santa Claus paper and tore a corner off to get her started.

In all of the chaos of the morning, neither Bernie nor I remembered to take photos. I didn't realize it until that night after we flopped into bed. I bolted upright and said, "We forgot to take pictures of Dani's first Christmas! She will never have a first Christmas again!" He looked at me like I was nuts. "Diane, which picture did you want? The one where she was running naked through the house like a crazy girl? The one with the red blotches all over her face from her crying fit? The one with the ornament in her mouth? The one with the little candy cane stuck in her hair? Or the one where she tried to eat Willie's clay?"

He was right. So, it wasn't a Hallmark Baby's First Christmas. It was our first Christmas with Dani, and we sure didn't need photos to remember it. As many occasions were with Dani, it would be pretty unforgettable. I lay back down and turned my head to look at him. "Video might have been fun, though." The very idea cracked us both up.

22

Tennessee

Life was so good in so many ways that we hardly noticed the clouds that were beginning to gather around the construction industry in Florida. A lot of Bernie's work was in condo conversion—developers purchased apartment buildings, converted them into condos, and sold them for about double the price per unit that they had paid. That boom began just before we moved to Florida, and Bernie had more work than he could handle. There were so many conversions—on top of new construction—that ultimately there was a glut, and that particular segment of Bernie's work had started to dry up.

He wasn't worried, or, if he was, he didn't tell me. Bernie is a craftsman carpenter. He does beautiful work, and there were always residential clients in between his commercial jobs for the big contractors. Thanks to his dad, there really wasn't anything in the construction field he couldn't do and nothing he wouldn't do to take care of his family.

We looked at it in the same way that we had come to look at the hurricane warnings we endured every season. If it didn't blow over—as most of them did—just batten down the hatches and ride it out. Bernie and I are not extravagant people, by any means. As single parents, we had both learned how to be frugal when it was necessary. We talked about the fact that work wasn't as plentiful as it had been, but we were prepared to batten down and ride it out.

But the new year brought more bad news. The Florida boom had definitely gone bust, like one of those fireworks that shoots off like a rocket, goes sky high, arcs, and then sputters back to earth, with nothing more than a fizzle.

The reality was that the cost of living in a resort community was so high that cutting back to everything except the necessities might not even be enough to get us through. Bernie was being practical, but I got upset every time he tried to bring up the possibility of moving back north. With all the maturity of a five-year-old, I wanted to stomp my feet, pound my fists, and shout, "It's not fair!"

When we first packed everything up and came to Florida, Bernie promised me that we would never move again, that we would be here forever. We believed we would eventually retire here, and we'd have a head start on all of the other snowbirds because we would be close to owning our house by then. For the first time in my life, I was in a neighborhood where I had made friends, put down roots, and gotten attached to the community, our church, and the neighbors.

We had worked hard to get where we were, and we didn't spend beyond our means. It didn't seem right. It wasn't Bernie's fault that the construction industry had tanked, but the whole mess was creating tension between us.

It didn't help matters when I pointed out to him what he already knew: that moving again would be hard on Willie and maybe harder still on Dani. She was in the first safe place of her life. What would it mean to uproot her and take her someplace entirely new and different? She was already enrolled in her second school in three years. It didn't take a professional educator or a child psychologist to suggest that changing schools again could have a very negative effect on what progress she was making.

I was determined to find a way not to uproot the family. Bernie was equally desperate to find work. We began discussing the possibility of his going back to Tennessee, where the construction industry was still strong. Condos were popping up like dandelions, and he had established residential clients there. Ryan was living in Tennessee, so Bernie could possibly bunk with him and his wife, Rene, while the kids and I stayed in Florida until the economy improved. I would try to pick up some more hours at the property management company, he would send most of his money back to me, and we'd ride it out. People did it all the time. It was no big deal, and if it could save us all from moving, it would be worth it. Bernie started to make calls up north, and we talked constantly about how we could make it work. Some nights I went to bed certain that everything would be fine, and other nights I tossed and turned till dawn, scrolling through every worst-case scenario.

There was virtually no work to be found in Florida, and it wore on us not only financially, but mentally and emotionally, especially on Bernie. He has been working since he was twelve years old. Work is who he is, and he was definitely not happy. He drove back to Tennessee a couple of times by himself to scout the lay of the land, and there were definitely a lot more opportunities there than in Florida. Each time he went to Tennessee, he did a couple of quick jobs and made enough money to get us through the next few months, but his absences were hard on all of us. Solo parenting "normal" kids is hard; solo parenting a special needs child was draining. Dani's outbursts increased when Bernie was gone, and Willie missed his dad terribly. My pipe dream of Bernie working in Tennessee and us staying in Florida and holding onto the house went up in smoke. Whatever we did, we were in it together, and we would do it as a family.

It broke my heart, but once the decision was made, all I could do was "Toughen up, buttercup," as Dorothy would say. We put our beloved dream house on the market.

To our surprise, there was immediate interest from several potential buyers, so we felt as if we needed to move quickly on finding something in Tennessee. Because we were familiar with Lebanon and Wilson County, we decided to look there, and in late April, we made a whirlwind weekend drive—900 miles north, 900 miles back south.

I told Bernie that if we were moving back to Tennessee, I wanted to buy a farm so we could provide a lot of our own food. If worse came to worst, at least we wouldn't go hungry. We told our real estate agent what we were looking for, but there was nothing in our price range at that time.

She found a log home that was on seven acres of land, on a dead-end street off a main road a few miles outside of Lebanon. It looked promising in the tiny photo and the write-up, but up close and in person, the house wasn't in good shape. And the ad failed to mention that the seven acres were seven acres of rocks—not exactly conducive to planting a garden, grazing animals, or digging an in-ground swimming pool.

There was a sign on the house next door, so we went to see that one. It was a fairly new brick house with three bedrooms, two baths, a good-size living room, a garage on the lower level of the house that had been semifinished into a family room, and no kitchen or floor coverings. Just a sub-floor. The seller who was fixing it up to put on the market had taken out all of the kitchen cabinets and appliances and pulled up the old carpet and tile to lay new carpet and tile.

Bernie saw potential. I saw disaster. Bernie saw a good price. I saw a money pit. We don't argue very often, but we had a showdown over this. He was drooling over the garage—a detached building— and pointed out that it was big enough to set up a carpentry shop.

I said that if he didn't get the house livable before he got a job, he could make his bedroom out there.

When the dust cleared, we agreed that if he would lay hardwood and tile and put in a kitchen before taking on outside work, we would buy it. As soon as we got back to Florida, Bernie took off back to Tennessee to monitor inspections on the house, call on some of his old clients, and generate some income to keep up with all of the outgo.

I started packing boxes, and as the stacks grew higher, Willie and I felt lower and lower. He didn't want to move. His whole life was there in Fort Myers Beach. He had been only four when we moved to Florida, and he really had no memory of Tennessee. His friends were here, his school, his church, and, of course, his surrogate grandparents Dorothy, Paul, Bill, and Doris. Willie asked me lots of questions—What was it like when Steven, Paul, and I had lived on the farm? What kind of animals would we get? Could we get a horse? Would we get snow? Where would he and Dani swim?

As much as we explained what we were doing and why to Dani, we had no way of knowing what she understood. She knew something was going on, and she didn't seem to like it. She hardly ate during the weekend that we drove up to Tennessee and back. I thought maybe she was carsick, but it continued a day or so afterward. For Dani not to eat, something had to be wrong.

It was worse when Bernie was gone. I was so frantic running to my job, taking care of two kids, doing all of the errands and shopping, and packing up the house that there wasn't any time left for playing. Bernie had always been the "fun parent." There's one in every family. I know Dani keenly felt his absence and missed his cuddles, kisses, and tickles.

Some of the notes from school pointed out that she seemed sad and lethargic, while on other days she was angry and in constant motion. One day Ms. Phipps wrote, "Better today, but still somewhat unfocused. I think she probably feels the change and it's hard for her with the packing and a parent gone."

I knew that, but there was nothing I could do. The one piece of good news we got was that the school finally found someone to do occupational therapy with Dani. It was important to have that in place so that when we got to Wilson County, that school district would have to do the same. Dani's days in school were very busy and maybe distracted her a bit from the change coming on. One day Ms. Phipps sent home a note saying, "Boy, she is developing a temper! That's good.:-)" I smiled back at the smiley face, glad for the oddly positive report on negative behavior.

When Bernie was able to come home for a long weekend, we spent the time doing all of the fun things we loved in Florida. We went to the beach, swam in our pool and the Kennys' pool, and rode bikes, and Willie drove Miss Dani in the little red jeep. We lingered even more than usual with neighbors on the evening dog walks and went as often as we could to Dorothy and

Dani on the beach with Dad.

Paul's so that Dani could jump on Amber's bed and watch sports on the sofa with Paul. Leaving Dorothy was going to be particularly hard on me. I looked at her as the mother I had always wanted. If I allowed myself to think about it, I could bawl my eyes out.

Bernie called Garet and Mr. O'Keefe to tell them we were moving to Tennessee. These were hard calls to make. Garet was out of state for the month visiting her family and was heartbroken that she couldn't come to say good-bye.

The people who were purchasing our house agreed to wait a couple of extra days to close so that Dani and Willie could finish out the school year. I had packed everything up by myself, and then Bernie flew down to load the rental truck, with some help from the neighbors. We had one last spaghetti dinner at Dorothy and Paul's the night before we left. We were going to pull out at the crack of dawn, so we had to say our good-byes that night. It was so hard. I felt lost, sad, and fearful. When Dani saw me crying, she came over and stood close beside me, leaning her head on my arm, which made me cry all the more.

As we drove off the island that morning, tears were streaming down my cheeks. We were all leaving a big part of ourselves behind, but I tried to convince myself that the best part of our lives was up ahead.

It was the road to get there that about did me in. Bernie drove the truck by himself. The passenger side of the cab was stacked with all of his tools and whatever else wouldn't fit in the cargo area. I was in the car with Willie, Dani, the three dogs, and Willie's parrot in the cage on the front passenger seat. If I got too close, or if the cage shifted toward me, that parrot bit me every chance she got. Whenever Willie dozed off in the backseat, I was sorely tempted to roll down the window and open the cage door.

Late afternoon on the second day we left, our caravan arrived safely in Tennessee—even the parrot. Ryan and his father-in-law came over to help, and together the five of us, including Willie, unloaded everything from the truck and the car into the garage, because there was still no flooring in the house. I asked them to put three mattresses in the house on the sub-floor in the living room, and I found the box with the linens. If we were going to be roughing it, we'd do it in the same room. I didn't want Dani or Willie to be frightened in their new home. Bernie put the mini-fridge we used to keep down by our pool in the future kitchen. I arranged our toiletries in the bathroom we would share, and Willie brought in the four small suitcases we would live out of until the floors were down, and we could move in the furniture. Home sweet home.

The good news was that since there was no kitchen, for a while I was off the hook when it came to cooking. "Where are we going for dinner, Bernie?" I could learn to like the sound of that.

In fact, the next couple of weeks were miserable on all of us. Dani missed the pool; in Florida she swam every day, sometimes twice a day. I'm sure she wondered why we didn't go to the beach anymore, where was Dorothy, where was Grandpa Bill, where were the manatees and the banana trees? I worried that sleeping on a mattress on a plywood floor in a virtually empty room would bring back bad memories for her and cause her to regress. Dani had been sleeping on the top mattress of her bed since the night we came home after the adoption in Tampa.

Luckily, that didn't seem to be a problem, so much as the long days with nothing to do while her mom and dad hammered and glued and shooed her away. I had set aside some of her toys, books, and DVDs in a separate bag, but I knew Dani was bored. And when she was bored, she got fidgety, which might escalate to bouncing off the walls and then exploding in a nuclear meltdown.

Hoping to ward off that ugliness, I broke frequently to take her, Willie, and the dogs for a walk in the small neighborhood. We never saw people outside, the humidity was horrendous, and everyone on this blue-collar street left for work early in the morning and was gone all day. There was no pool to jump into, to cool off. The road we lived on wasn't like the paved, flat streets in Laguna Shores. Dani had such a hard time riding her bike that she grew frustrated one day, got off, and left it in the middle of the street, where it rolled down the hill and into someone's yard. I told her to go get the bike, but she was having none of it. I really couldn't blame her. My attitude wasn't much better. I handed the dog leashes to Willie and went to retrieve the bike. Dani walked on ahead of us back to the house. Ms. Phipps's observation echoed in my head. "Boy, she is developing a temper! That's good." It wasn't feeling so good to me at the moment.

Finally, Bernie had all of the floors down except the kitchen, so we could start moving in the furniture that had been in the garage/ workshop for two weeks. Bernie and I carried in Dani's armoire and bed while she and Willie were watching a movie, and she didn't notice. My plan was to recreate Dani's room exactly as it had been in Florida, so I asked Bernie to take her to do some errands and pick up some lunch, and I enlisted Willie to help me. He has a better memory than I do and would remember what went where, down to every stuffed animal.

Willie is a hard worker and meticulous, so within an hour, Dani's bedroom was an exact replica of the one we had left behind in Florida, from the tile and the rugs on the floor to the prints on the wall and the shades for the windows. The Hello Kitty com- forter, the pillows, and probably fifty stuffed animals were sprung from the boxes they had been confined in for the last two weeks and were happily in their places on her bed and the top shelf of her bookcase, which was filled with her favorite books.

Willie stood on the front porch waiting for his father and sister to drive up the street. When he saw the car, he opened the door and hollered to me, "They're home!"

Bernie knew what we had been doing while they were gone, and he wasted no time getting Dani inside. I was already in her bedroom because I wanted to see her face when she first saw it.

The way she had been moping around the house the last few weeks, I so much needed to see her smile, anything that would let me know that maybe we hadn't completely ruined her life by taking her out of her comfort zone.

I heard Willie say, "Dani, we have a surprise for you. Here, hold my hand and come with me." Their footsteps echoed through the empty living room and down the hall. Willie had his hands gently over her eyes as he guided her to the door. He took them away, and as she saw her room, her entire face lit up exactly as it had the day a year ago when we brought her home for the first time and she saw her own girlie bedroom. Just as she did that day, she leaped onto her bed, hugged her Hello Kitty pillow, and laughed for joy.

Then she did something she had never done before. She patted the bed beside her and said, "Buh . . . buh . . . buh . . . buh. Buh . . . buh . . . buh . . . buh." The three of us looked at her, looked at one another, and repeated what she said back to her. "Buh . . . buh . . . buh . . . buh? Buh . . . buh . . . buh . . . buh?" It was Willie who shouted, "Book? You want a book?" She smiled and patted the bed again. "Buh . . . buh . . . buh . . . buh." Willie scrambled to find her favorite, sat beside her, opened the book, and began to read. "Brown bear, brown bear, what do you see? I see a red bird looking at me." As Willie said "red bird," Dani patted the bird, and I believed my heart would burst.

23

The Public Eye

While we were still living in Florida, Bernie got a call out of the blue from a woman with the Children's Board of Hillsborough County. The Children's Board is an umbrella agency for lots of children's services and parenting education programs. It was the agency that put on the Heart Gallery event at GameWorks in Tampa where we first saw Dani's photo.

The woman in charge of communications, Carolyn Eastman, told Bernie that a reporter from the *St. Petersburg Times* was interested in doing a story on successful adoptions and wanted to know if we would participate. She told Bernie it would just be a paragraph or two on each family, and that they planned to publish it around Valentine's Day, hoping to motivate people to become adoptive parents.

Bernie told her he would talk it over with me. It went over like a brick. I said, "No, thank you!" I didn't want to be in the newspaper. I had never even had any of my weddings listed in the paper. We were not public-eye kind of people in any way, shape, or form.

I told Bernie there were hundreds of other families in Florida who could do it and probably wanted to do it, so we didn't need to. We were having financial issues and job insecurity and were fighting with Dani's school to get the occupational therapy we knew it was obligated to give her. I didn't feel as if we needed to add one more thing to our plates.

He told Carolyn Eastman, but she was persistent and called him again a week later. She thought our story was so moving and inspirational. I didn't see how it was any more inspirational than anyone else's, and Bernie didn't either. But he pointed out that if it weren't for the Heart Gallery, we wouldn't have Dani at all. I could tell he was softening, but I stood my ground.

He called Carolyn Eastman back and gave her my number, and one of her staff members called me the next day. Thanks, but no thanks, I said.

So she called me herself. There is a reason Carolyn Eastman is in charge of communications. She definitely has a gift for it. She told me more about the Children's Board and what it does and about what an impact the Heart Gallery has had on finding "forever families," as they are called. I listened while I folded clothes and kept an eye on the clock.

She told me that although she had met Danielle only once, she had been unforgettably touched. I knew lots of people felt that way about Dani. There was something about her that made an immediate impression on people and made them want to help her.

Then Carolyn told me her personal story, why she felt so passionate about adoption and why she felt so drawn to our story. "I was in foster care myself before being adopted by my foster family. My foster mother actually worked for our sister agency in St. Pete for twenty years, so I know this world well. Both of my daughters are adopted. I have traveled this path my whole life, and working here is the way I give back.

"I remember when Danielle first came into care because a good friend of mine called me to sound off about the case, she was so upset over it. Garet really pushed for Danielle to be included in the Heart Gallery. She took the lead on it, as she did with everything else. You know that Garet is adopted, too?" Carolyn asked. I didn't respond, so she continued, "When I first saw Danielle in the Heart Gallery photo, I thought she looked very sweet. But I knew how great her needs were and how much care she would need, so I don't know that I was as optimistic as Garet was. She always believed Danielle would find a family.

"My girls like to look through the Heart Gallery photographs and pick a child to pray for, pray that the child will get a home just as they did. It personalizes the photos for them. They've done it since they were itty-bitty. Out of all the photos, they chose Danielle and prayed for her to find a family. Something about her spoke to them, too. I didn't find out until later that Danielle was the child I had heard about.

"As I told Bernie, this is such an amazing story. I know it will touch people and hopefully motivate some of them to adopt, too."

That was some sales pitch. I had stopped folding clothes and was sitting on the sofa, blown away by what she had told me. I knew Garet was adopted, but it was unbelievable that Carolyn and her girls were, too. Bernie and I had always felt that finding Dani and bringing her home was part of God's plan, but this was bigger than we realized. It occurred to me that maybe adopting Dani wasn't the end of God's plan for us.

If that was so, how could I possibly say no? Besides, I told myself, it wasn't such a big deal. A couple of paragraphs in a story that would be old news within twenty-four hours.

I told Carolyn it had to be on a weekend so that Bernie wouldn't have to take off work and the kids would be home from school.

She called me back within an hour and asked if the coming weekend would work. We didn't have any plans set in stone—we had cut back pretty dramatically on entertainment and were sticking close to home. She said the reporter was Lane DeGregory, whom she had worked with several times and trusted completely. The same with the photographer, Melissa Lyttle. Carolyn was going to come along, and Garet wanted to come, too, so she could see us and visit with Dani.

Before the adoption, Garet had come down to Fort Myers Beach a couple of times to check on Dani because she was her adoption case manager. But her connection with Dani wasn't only professional. Garet had loved Dani as soon as she met her at Tampa General Hospital and had made a promise that against all odds, she would find Dani a home.

The first time Garet came to check on her, though, Dani got so upset she had a major meltdown. We were all confused, especially Garet. We thought Dani would be so happy to see her. We didn't figure out until after Garet left that Dani was afraid Garet was taking her back to the foster home because that was what had always happened when Garet picked her up.

Before Garet came the next time, we assured Dani that Garet was not coming to take her away but to play, and she was much calmer during the second visit. By the time Garet left, they were old friends again.

The Saturday of the interview I got Dani up early to leave plenty of time to get her hair brushed out and pulled into a ponytail and twist her favorite pink hair ornament around it to match her pink shirt. After breakfast I sent her and Willie outside to play so that the house would stay clean.

Bernie was out in the yard keeping an eye on the kids, and he yelled up to me from the first floor when the four women got there.

Garet squatted down in between Dani and Willie with an arm around each child's shoulder. The photographer was easy to pick out—she was the one with the camera, and the reporter was the one with the notebook. Bernie was talking to the other lady, who had to be Carolyn. She held her hand out and introduced herself, thanked Bernie and me for agreeing to participate in the story, and introduced us to Lane and Melissa.

"I was telling Bernie that when we pulled up to your house, we saw a little boy and girl playing in the driveway. I assumed the boy was Willie," Carolyn said, smiling at Willie, "and I remarked to Garet how nice it was that Danielle had another girl her age living in the neighborhood to play with. Garet laughed at me and said, 'That's Dani.' I was flabbergasted! She has grown a foot! When I last saw her, she was brunette and so pale, so lethargic. Now look at her! She's a blonde! It's like a light has turned on inside her. She is unrecognizable."

The grown-ups sat at the kitchen table while Dani and Willie went back to play in the backyard. I told Melissa I would prefer that she not take pictures of the kids unless Bernie or I were there. I didn't know the reporter or the photographer, and I was still wary of allowing them too much access. I was nervous enough about talking to Lane.

We had never been interviewed before, so we had no idea what to expect, but it was easier having Garet and Carolyn there. It made us feel more as if we were sitting around talking with friends, and Lane did her best to put us at ease.

Melissa wanted a picture of the four of us together, and I warned her that Dani didn't always like having her photo taken, so it would have to be quick.

Naturally, Dani made a liar of me. Bernie had his hand on one of her arms, while I held onto the other so that she wouldn't run off or get wiggy, which was what she normally did. I don't know what it was about Melissa, but while she got off a bunch of shots, Dani stood still, not exactly smiling but at least looking into the camera. I asked Melissa whether we might get some copies. So far, all of our attempts at family portraits at church had been thwarted by Dani's obstinacy.

Melissa took some more candid shots while we chatted in the driveway. I was pretty much done with being interviewed and knew that if we went back into the house, we'd be sitting there another two hours. I was almost wishing that Dani would throw a fit and drive everyone off, but she was being as good as gold. I asked the women if they'd like a bottle of water for the road, and they got the hint. Garet gave Willie and Dani big hugs. I know she missed seeing Dani on a regular basis. Since the adoption, Garet was no longer on the case. Bernie was good about keeping in touch with her and Mr. O'Keefe, but it wasn't the same as seeing her.

Lane called the next week to thank us for meeting with them, then told us that she, Carolyn, Melissa, and Garet had talked about the story all the way back to St. Pete. She wondered if we might be agreeable to her and Melissa coming back the next weekend to talk to us some more. I wasn't crazy about the idea, but I felt that if they were willing to drive three hours down and three hours back to talk to us again, I guessed we could give them another hour. I asked what happened to running the story on Valentine's Day, and she said they had decided that Mother's Day would be more suitable.

We cleared another Saturday, talked at the kitchen table, then went outside to take some more photos, mostly of Dani. She had inexplicably developed a love of the camera, and Willie—who had a keen interest in photography—stuck to Melissa like glue.

While Melissa was shooting, Lane asked whether they could come back on a school day to see what Dani's regular routine was like. Bernie looked skeptical. "Don't you have enough for a couple of paragraphs by now?" Lane said that when she had filled her editors in on the first visit with us, they all agreed that there was a lot more to the story than a couple of paragraphs could do justice to. I felt a red flag go up, and so did Bernie. "So, what are you talking about then, Lane?"

She explained that they would like to do a feature focused entirely on Dani, with more photos, to run around Mother's Day. Bernie and I looked at each other, and he read my mind. "You know, Diane and I agreed to a couple of paragraphs as part of an article to call attention to adoption. This is much bigger than that. We'll need to talk about this and sleep on it. We'll give you a call on Monday."

I could see that Lane and Melissa were disappointed and maybe a little surprised. They were probably more accustomed to people wanting to be in the newspaper, instead of the other way around.

The next day at church, we asked our pastor and his wife for help in making a decision, especially about our discomfort with tooting our own horn and violating Dani's privacy. Were we being fair to her? Was the story going to make her look like some kind of freak?

We all talked it over, and we prayed over it. We asked ourselves, "If only one family is inspired by our story to adopt just one child, would that be worth it?" Thinking of what might have been Dani's fate if we had not been led to her, there was no other answer but yes. It would be worth it. We prayed that Lane and Melissa would honor our trust, that no one would be hurt, that one child might be saved, and we decided to go forward with the story.

Lane and Melissa came to talk to us a couple more times and shot more photos and even some video. We had given our permission for Lane to talk to Dani's speech therapist at school during one of her sessions with Dani because we trusted Leslie implicitly. She was nearly as protective of Dani as we were.

Lane told us she was talking to people in Tampa who had been part of the story before us, such as Detective Holste, the physicians at Tampa General, and Dr. Armstrong at USF. The more she said, the more anxious we got. Then she mentioned Michelle Crockett, and Bernie and I both froze. It didn't occur to us that Lane might talk to her, and Bernie especially got upset. "I don't want to know any more about it than I already know. Why are you giving her any attention? She doesn't deserve anything but jail."

Lane was taken aback. She said that one of her editors had asked if she had tracked down the birth mother and whether she was going to get Michelle Crockett's side of the story. "Her side of the story? She has no side of the story!" Bernie was incensed. I rarely saw him lose his temper, but Michelle Crockett's name was bound to do it. Lane said she would talk to her editor and let him know our feelings.

Mother's Day came and went, and there was no story, but by then we were so wrapped up in selling our home, looking for a house in Tennessee, and preparing for the move that it was the furthest thing from our minds. About two months after we had moved into the Gilbert Valley house, Lane called Bernie one evening right before dinner, and he put his cell on speaker phone so that we could both hear and talk to her.

She told us that it had turned into something much bigger, not just the length of the story, but its presentation. That it was actually going to be a "multi-media package." I asked her what that meant. Lane explained that in addition to the print story, there would be audio, a slide show, and even some video on the website. We knew that we had been recorded, and we knew Melissa had a small video camera, but it didn't occur to me that there would be anything but a story in the actual newspaper. I was definitely not media-savvy.

I think Lane was trying to prepare us for the size of the story, especially since we were so reluctant in the first place. Then she told us that she had also spoken to Michelle Crockett, and the birth mother was included in the story.

My heart sank, and my stomach knotted. "We asked you not to talk to her," Bernie said, his voice very testy. Lane said that her editors had insisted on "balance," and if she had not given the mother the opportunity to speak, the story likely would have been pulled. Honestly, that would have been fine by us.

Bernie asked Lane when it was going to run, and she said in a couple of days. She could probably hear me gulp over phone.

She told us she would make sure we were e-mailed the copy before that and that she hoped we would feel as if it had been worth it.

As it turned out, we didn't get the copy until the night before it was supposed to run. I sat down in front of the computer, with Bernie looking over my shoulder. It was even more nerve-wracking to read than I thought it would be. It's so unsettling to see your life spread out in public like that. Some of the things we said sounded pretty goofy in print, others I couldn't remember at all, and we worried that some of what had been written about Dani when we first met her might embarrass her. Did the fact that she couldn't read the article and in fact wasn't even aware of its existence make it any less of an invasion of her privacy or more?

The first thing that I read made me cringe. "Part One: The Feral Child." It reminded me of when we first saw Dani's photo at the Heart Gallery and the social workers suggested we look up the term. I know it is used to describe children like Dani and other children who are much worse—like the boy raised in the woods with wolves or the girl raised by dogs—although Dr. Perry had once written that those children have an advantage over severely neglected children, because they have at least been nurtured by something. But the word just sounds ugly and dirty, and "feral" is not at all how we ever saw Dani, even at her worst. Yet there it was, in bold print for everyone to read. We felt as if the word was used to grab people's attention and was sensationalizing, and that seemed to be a slight to Dani.

Bernie was very impressed by Detective Holste and said he was going to call the Plant City Police Department to thank him for the role he played in saving Dani.

I was glad Lane had talked to Mr. O'Keefe, though I know he really didn't want to talk to her. And Leslie Goldenberg said nice things. We smiled at what Dr. Armstrong said about her first impression of Dani: "My hope was that she would be able to sleep through the night, to be out of diapers, and to feed herself. . . . If things went really well, Danielle would end up in a nice nursing home." It was good to know we had already surpassed those expectations.

And then we came to the part with Michelle Crockett—"Part Three: The Mother." Bernie walked away. He has said all along that he doesn't want to know anything about her; that the past is the past, Dani is with us now, and that's all that matters.

I'll admit to some curiosity but from a psychological point of view—how could any mother do this to her child? She had cared for her two boys; how could she have done this to her own flesh and blood?

Michelle was still living in Plant City, in a mobile home with her boys near where she had lived previously. According to the story, the trailer was clean, which was surprising, considering the appalling conditions of the shack Dani had lived in.

It's impossible to know where, if anywhere, Michelle Crockett was telling the truth. She admitted to meeting a man in a casino whose name she couldn't recall—Ron, or maybe Bob—and going back to his hotel room. She claimed that she took Dani out for pizza once, to the park, and to the library, but she couldn't remember where they were or the names of the places.

She actually showed Lane copies of the abuse reports from 2002 but only because she thought that they proved that she was not an unfit mother, because the DCF did not remove Dani either time. She claimed that she was "shocked when the police took Danielle out of my house that day."

Maybe the reason she was able to do what she did to Dani was because she lived in such denial; she refused to accept responsibility for anything. It was all someone else's fault, everything happened to her and not because of her. It made me sick but not as sick as I felt when I read that she and her sons had sneaked into the hospital the day after Dani was taken into custody and taken a photo of her in her hospital gown. Michelle showed it to Lane; I hate that Michelle even has this photo. That she's not in jail is a travesty.

There were a couple of inaccuracies I definitely wanted to be taken care of. For one, the story said that the reason we adopted was because I couldn't have any more children. That's not true. We just knew we couldn't do any better than Willie, so we stopped there. We had always told him this when he was little and would ask for a baby brother or sister. And it was true. We couldn't do any better than our sweet Willie.

The other inaccuracy was more upsetting. Lane wrote that when Dani came, we moved Willie into the laundry room, squeezing a daybed between the washing machine and Dani's rocking horse. That was totally untrue. Poor Willie! He had actually been in the biggest bedroom in the house, the one that Paul and Steven had shared when we first moved into that house. The room had two single beds that had been theirs, and neither one was squeezed up beside the washing machine! It was true that Willie sometimes got scared down there, but he was the one who came up with the walkie-talkie idea, and he went upstairs to sleep any time that he was anxious. We knew he would grow out of it and eventually, as a teenager, would cherish his privacy on the lower level—as well as his easy access to the pool.

When we called Lane about those two things, she told us that the story had already been printed because it was a special package. I pointed out the errors, and she apologized and said they would be corrected in the online version. But meanwhile, readers would come to believe we were monsters for squeezing poor Willie into a laundry room, too scared to sleep. For the first time since we had moved, I was glad we weren't living in Florida, and I wouldn't have to hide my face in the grocery store for being a terrible mother.

The story went online the night of July 31 and was published in the paper on August 1, 2008.

Bernie and I e-mailed friends and members of the family to warn them. "Hello, everyone. Danielle's story hit the *St. Petersburg*

Times website tonight. She is 'The Girl in the Window' story. Willie does NOT sleep in the laundry room, he has his own room! I don't know where that came from! Dani continues to progress. A couple weeks ago she said 'reee' and handed mom a book to read to her. Thanks for all your prayers and encouragement! We miss you all!"

Carolyn Eastman had told us that stories about the Heart Gallery and successful adoptions always generated a big response and lots of interest. But nothing could have prepared us for the reaction "The Girl in the Window" got.

Within forty-eight hours of the story being online, the paper's website crashed because of all of the hits. They got it back up, and it crashed again.

I had never paid attention to reader comments before. I hardly knew they existed, but these were at the bottom of the story, so I started to read them. The first came in before the paper was on the stands, at 1:09 a.m. on August 1. "Anonymous" gave credit to the DCF for doing something right. I was surprised, considering that the DCF left Dani in that house three years longer than it should have.

Five comments later, another "anonymous" said that it wasn't right that we were "making William sleep in the laundry room next to the washer and it sounds like he was being a little abused." I got mad all over again about not being able to fact-check the story.

I read on. Most people expressed outrage at Michelle, heartbreak over what Dani had gone through, and gratitude that she was in a safe place now. I had to stop reading, though, after about the fifth mention of Willie being in the laundry room. It was maddening, but there was nothing we could do about it.

The paper and Hillsborough Kids were being inundated with calls from people wanting to know how to help. Other members of the media called the Heart Gallery looking for us. It was the second time in two days that I was glad we were at a relatively safe distance from the hullabaloo. If we had still been in Florida, we probably couldn't have left our house.

Carolyn called us to see what she could do to help, and I nearly cried in relief. She asked if we might consider setting up a website for Dani, which would take some of the traffic away from the paper and the Children's Board and the Heart Gallery. She really stepped in for us, finding someone from a graphics company in Tampa to donate his time to design and create the site. We talked to people at the graphics company a couple of times, they got permission from Melissa to use some photos, and within days "Dani's Story" was up. The owner of the company was so touched by the story that he decided he wanted to adopt, and we advised him on what to expect and how to work the system.

That helped us process everything. We had said all along that if hearing our story inspired just one person to adopt, then it was worth going public with it. There was one, and we felt as if a prayer had been answered.

People started coming to the website as soon as the paper added a link to it on "The Girl in the Window" story. There were also links to child abuse hotlines, the Heart Gallery, and information on how to foster. We asked the designer to put links to the Heart Gallery on Dani's home page as well. I imagined hundreds of people going to those sites who never would have without the story, and the laundry-room issue shrunk to its appropriate size, compared with the enormousness of what this story had done.

On Dani's website, the designer had added a link so that readers could send e-mails to us. This was better than an address or a phone number. We decided to connect it to Bernie's e-mail address because he never uses it. Mine is full of everything from family news to school things to goat sales.

The first time Bernie checked his e-mail after the website was up, he yelled, "Holy cow! What is going on?" He sat dumbfounded in front of the computer. There were dozens and dozens of e-mails. Bernie went from getting maybe one e-mail a week from Bass Pro Shops to hundreds. We felt as if we had to answer every one, but we were just completely overwhelmed.

It got even crazier after the story was picked up by other papers in Florida and I guess around the country and then the world, because we were getting e-mails through Dani's website from everywhere, places I had never heard of in my life. The senders ran the gamut from people who had special needs kids of their own and wanted us to know how much they related to us, to people who had never had children but were moved by our story. We heard from people who promised to pray and light a candle for us. We heard from friends of relatives, relatives of friends, and friends of friends. We heard from people who had "cures" and suggested links, books, and websites. We heard from teachers who had collected cards from their students and wanted to send them to Willie and Dani, from professors who wanted to use the story as a teaching tool in their classes, and from grandmas who wanted to sew quilts for the kids.

We even got an e-mail from a young woman who offered to babysit for free, which practically made me reach through the computer to hug her. We had never even tried to find a sitter, knowing that any normal person would run for her life once she heard the job description. Back in Florida, the Kennys and the LaPiccolas had been happy to have Dani in their own houses for an hour or so, if I really needed to get something done, but we barely knew any of our neighbors on Gilbert Valley Road.

Lots of college students contacted us, explaining that they were studying children with special needs and wondering whether they could interview us about Dani. I wrote back to all of them and answered as many of their questions as I could, either via e-mail or on the phone. We also heard from students who had been inspired to change their majors to do something that would help children, and that was very gratifying.

There were many media inquiries. We heard from an editor with the Readers Digest Association, and because we were fans of *Readers Digest*, we were open to the magazine's proposal. The editor wanted to condense and reprint Lane's article with Melissa's photos and do a short follow-up interview with us. Their focus would be on faith and inspiring others to open their hearts to fostering or adopting.

On the other hand, we were also contacted by a national television show that was famous for its ugly confrontations between its guests. The producers either wanted us to appear on the show with Michelle Crockett or observe from a studio while they confronted her on camera. We were appalled that they would think for a minute that we were the kind of people who might do that. They kept asking the same question in different ways, but our answer remained no.

And then that fall along came Oprah. One of the producers who worked for *The Oprah Winfrey Show* contacted Carolyn, who knew her from her earlier work as a local news anchor. Because Carolyn trusted her passion and professionalism, she put the producer in touch with us, and, over several months, we came to trust her as well.

I had never seen Oprah's show, but it was nothing personal. I rarely watched television and never during the day. The show was on either when I was running to get kids to school, taking them to something, or marshalling their homework assignments. But you would have had to be living under a rock on Mars during the last twenty years not to know how crazy popular Oprah's show was. The power of her influence and the vast size of her audience could really make an incredible impact on the issues we felt so strongly about.

But in just the brief amount of time since the *St. Petersburg Times* article had run, we knew how media attention could turn our lives upside down and how much of an invasion of our family's privacy it could be. We felt enormous pressure to weigh the merits of the former with the disadvantages of the latter.

We didn't have our pastor in Florida to turn to, and we didn't really know anyone in Tennessee, so we had many frank conversations with Carolyn and relied on her to help us through.

The producers had several thoughts on how to handle the story, but what we wanted more than anything was to make clear the damage that Dani and other children like her suffer from the extreme neglect inflicted on them—not only by their families but compounded by tragically dysfunctional children's services agencies. We did not want drama—which meant no appearance by Michelle Crockett. And no live interviews with Dani.

We wanted viewers to see how far she had come and how much difference love and attention had made in her life. We wanted viewers to see how much she had had an impact on our lives. But our primary goal was to raise awareness of the needs of children in the foster care system, right here in America, and to convey the joys and rewards of adopting.

The producers of the *Oprah* show were very open to our concerns, and when they told us that Dr. Bruce Perry—an expert in the field of severe child neglect—was going to be a guest on the show, we agreed to do it. We hoped that we would have an opportunity before or after the taping to sit and talk with him privately about Dani.

Once we said yes, things moved quickly. We spent a little more than twenty-four hours in Chicago, but we made the most of it. Willie's favorite part of the whole experience was the limos. One came all the way to Lebanon to pick us up, then took us to the Nashville airport. We had never ridden in one before. We were so naïve, we wouldn't let Willie have a bottle of water because we thought we would have to buy it, and we were saving our cash for Chicago, not knowing what we would be responsible for there, either.

The plane ride was uneventful. Dani looked out the window, but she didn't seem to think it was all that unusual to be flying through and above the clouds. She liked the cup of juice and the bag of pretzels the best. At the Chicago airport, we were picked up by another car; the driver was so friendly that when we told him it was our first time in Chicago, he drove us all over the city and pointed out all of the sites. I was leaning out the window like a total hick, taking pictures of buildings. We definitely felt like "country comes to town." I don't think Willie's mouth closed during the entire ride.

After we settled into our rooms, Dr. Perry called to introduce himself and tell us how much he was looking forward to meeting us. I had read so much about his work with children that it was as much of a thrill to meet him as it was going to be to meet Oprah.

The next morning when we were having breakfast in the hotel dining room, Dr. Perry came in from his run and joined us for coffee, so he got to observe Dani for about twenty minutes. She was doing so well—using her fork, drinking out of a cup, sitting still beside Bernie. Just as Dr. Perry remarked on how well she had attached to us and how comfortable she seemed, I saw her eyes turn to an elderly couple sitting across the room from us. She popped up, walked very deliberately over to their table, and plopped on the banquette beside the woman, looking at her as if to say, "Well, what are you going to feed me?" Dr. Perry was laughing and asked if she did that a lot. I told him no, but that the couple probably reminded her of the elderly friends we had left behind in Florida, whom we all missed so much. He seemed impressed that Dani had made real attachments to people. Bernie and I have always maintained that she does not suffer from attachment disorder, which many people presume.

The taping of the show went by in a blur and about six hours after we walked off the set and got in the car to take us to the airport, we were back in our simple little home in Tennessee. I scrubbed off my makeup, changed into jeans and a sweatshirt, fed the dogs, and made lunches for the next day, while Bernie got

Dani showered, into her pajamas, and settled down on her bed with Lullaby Gloworm. I sat on Willie's bed as he said his prayers, and I kissed him goodnight. I picked his dirty clothes up off the floor, stopped in the bathroom to pick up Dani's, and went downstairs to the laundry room. Back to reality. Thank God.

On the day the show aired, Willie, Bernie and I sat down to watch it in the family room. Since it wasn't *Sponge Bob* or *Sesame Street*, Dani had absolutely no interest and went off to her room to play.

It is a very strange and surreal experience to watch yourself on television. The show started with segments about some pretty infamous cases of children who had been severely neglected. Then there Bernie and I were on stage in a semi-circle with Dr. Perry and Oprah. I remember thinking it would be cheesy to hold Bernie's hand so the two of us sat there looking stiff as boards.

In between talking to us, the producers inserted pre-taped interviews with Detective Holste, Garet White, and Lane DeGregory, and Oprah Skyped with Dr. Armstrong. Oprah asked us questions about Dani, about our home life, our hopes for her, and what we wanted people to know. I had totally forgotten everything that we had said and what had been said to us while we taped the show, so it was interesting to actually sit and take it all in. We sounded smart enough, even if we did look like deer in the headlights!

It was especially gratifying to hear Dr. Armstrong and Dr. Perry talk about how we instinctively knew how to care for Dani—allowing her to be a baby, making her feel loved and safe, and helping her learn and progress. I guess "instinctively" meant "not professionally." That didn't bother me. They were not judging us, by any means. In fact, they were very kind in their observations and very encouraging. When Oprah asked Dr. Perry what advice he would give us, he kind of smiled and shook his head. "Just keep doing what you're doing because it's working." Coming from someone with his experience and reputation, those words just made me tear up, and Bernie patted my knee.

The only comic relief came at the end of the show, when Oprah was talking about what a great big brother Willie had been and what a "remarkable young man" he must be and then asked for him to come out and join us on set.

When Willie was led to the stage he didn't look nearly as terrified as we did, just totally confused and maybe a little bit nervous that he might be in trouble. He climbed up onto the platform, and Oprah grabbed him and put him in her lap. His feet dangled above the floor, his eyes popped as wide as saucers, and a blush rose in his cheeks. I glanced over at him sitting on the sofa on the other side of Bernie and he was blushing again!

Oprah shared with him that she had been telling the audience (and the millions now watching at home with us) what a special boy he was and how much she admired him for everything he did for Dani. On camera, Willie looked even more puzzled, simply shrugged his shoulders, and remained mute. As Oprah wrapped up the show, she leaned over and asked Willie if he would say good-bye. "Good-bye," he squeaked.

Three days after the show aired,, Carolyn Eastman sent us an e-mail. "Just wanted to be sure you folks knew this. Dani's site has received more than 45,000 visitors since the *Oprah* show ran!" I called Bernie over to see. "45,000 visitors?" he exclaimed. "Let's hope they all don't send us an e-mail!"

24

Big Brother

Though our family and friends were initially enthusiastic about our desire to adopt a child, when the semi-formed idea became the reality of a child like Dani and all of the issues and the challenges she carried with her, they became concerned. Some were quite vehemently outspoken also. Even our pastor told us that if we had any doubts, God would not look unkindly on us if we changed our minds.

As usual, Dorothy was the most outspoken, predicting that the demands of taking care of someone like Dani would ruin not only our lives, but Willie's, too. That seemed a bit overly dramatic to Bernie and me, but we appreciated her honesty. Yet we didn't wander into this blindly. From the time we first saw Dani's photo at the Heart Gallery event and learned of her condition, we talked it up one side and down the other, night after night.

We shared everything with Willie. We were as honest as we could be in letting him know that Dani would not be the kind of little sister or brother he had imagined. The one he would toss a ball with, race his bike against, vie with to see who ran the fastest and jumped the highest, helped with homework, the one he would share everything with—secrets, jokes, tricks, and fears. Dani would not be that sibling.

If at any point in the process of the adoption, Willie had come to us and asked us not to do it, we would have stopped. Nothing would have been worth hurting our sweet boy, the one child whose creation we shared. But we were pretty certain that wouldn't happen because we knew enough about the character of our son to know that he would respond in exactly the way he did—with unconditional love.

Willie was born with that nurturing gene, which was passed along from Bernie and me as surely as his blue eyes and small frame were. All of our boys have it, but in none of the four is nurturing as inherent to his character as it is to Willie's.

That empathy for others was a big part of what drew me to Bernie, particularly after my two marriages to rather self-absorbed men. Not long after Bernie and I became friends, but before we were dating, we were driving back to the contractor's office from working on a job together. It had been a yucky day, cold and drizzling, and we were dead on our feet. All I could think about was home and a hot shower before making dinner for Paul, Steven, and me. We passed a park, and Bernie noticed an elderly man sort of aimlessly walking about, not dressed for the weather.

There might as well have been a bumper sticker on the back of his truck. "I brake for hurt animals, lost children, senior citizens, and anyone in need." He made a U-turn in the middle of the road, and we drove back to the park. Bernie got out of the truck and carefully approached the gentleman so as not to startle him. It was clear that the man was not homeless but had wandered off from wherever he was supposed to be and, sadly, could not remember where that was. Bernie took off his own jacket to put on the man and urged him to get into the truck with us. Bernie asked him questions, trying to figure out where he might belong, but all that the man knew was that it was a place with other people. We drove to a service station to get a Yellow Pages, and we looked up assisted-living places. Thankfully, we were still in Tennessee and not in Florida, or we would have been driving around for days.

There was a senior citizens' center not too far away, so we drove there, and both of us walked in with the man. It turned out that he had not walked off from the center, but the folks there knew him. They suspected that he had left his home on foot, heading to the center, and had lost his way. They promised to get him safely home and thanked us profusely. That incident showed me the man Bernie Lierow is. He wasn't doing it to impress me, and he didn't ask whether it was okay. Helping others, taking the literal shirt off his back, came as instinctually to him as breathing, and that not only filled me with admiration for him but played a big role in moving our relationship to something more serious.

I was always the person to take in the blind dog with the broken leg that was left on the side of the road; to love the broken, dirty doll more than the most beautiful one in the display case; to sit at lunch in the cafeteria with the kid whom the others left out. Our need to nurture extended even to houses. Bernie and I were both drawn to rundown, abandoned buildings that we were sure just needed a little TLC—supplemented by huge amounts of elbow grease and manual labor—to be restored to their proud and dignified selves.

Willie's personality was nothing out of the ordinary in our family. In fact, it was quite normal. If he had reacted in any other way, we would have wondered where the heck we had gone wrong and whose child he was!

We were so very proud of him. We always hear parents boasting about their "gifted" children, and we usually nod and smile at them. Willie worked hard but struggled academically because of his ADHD and a reading disorder, and his size means he will never be a star athlete—or even a competitive one. But he is supremely gifted in the ways that matter the most to us, and he is everything that a little girl—any little girl—could wish for in a big brother: protective, patient, kind, thoughtful, helpful, entertaining, strong, and loving.

The first time Willie met Dani in her classroom at Sanders Elementary, he was afraid of her. We could see it in his face, and he later admitted it was true. That room alone was a lot to take in, especially for a young boy who had never been exposed to anything like the children in Mr. O'Keefe's care. But Willie didn't run from it. Instead, he spent the few hours we were there picking up toys that other children dropped, reading stories, and helping the teacher aides. He kept an eye on Dani but didn't get too close to her. He sat beside her at the lunch table but didn't try to feed her. Maybe he was afraid she would bite! But as we were telling her good-bye, he chimed in, and the empathy he had for her was evident in his voice.

When we got in the car, it was Paul who was weeping. It was Willie who had one question: "When is she going to come visit us?"

We believe Willie bonded with Dani subconsciously the minute we came into the classroom when she grasped him by the forearms and stared deeply into his eyes before running away, squawking. It simply took the rest of him a few hours to catch up with the part of him that she had already touched. Once that happened, he never had a second thought, and loving Dani became as natural to him as loving us, his stepbrothers, his dogs, and that annoying parrot.

Readers of the newspaper story were especially touched with Willie's answer to Lane's question about Dani taking up so much of our time: "She needs them more than me." I don't think Willie has ever really felt deprived of our time, attention, or love since Dani came. He is not getting less of that since she came to live with us. As any parent who worries about finding enough love or time for a second child—or a third, a fourth, a fifth, or a sixth—knows, the well is bottomless when it comes to your children.

I think that seeing Willie drive Dani around in that little red jeep, and how much he loved being that guy for her, convinced Dorothy that everything would be all right between the two of them.

The only time I have ever seen Willie get even a little upset over something Dani received that he didn't was when we were able to get her signed up for therapeutic horse riding at the Naples Equestrian Center. Her sessions were once a week, and we all went together. I could see the longing on Willie's face as Dani sat on the horse and was led around the rink. Willie has always loved horses and wanted so much to ride, but the program was only for special needs children. Lessons for non-special needs kids were well out of our reach financially, especially during the last few months of the time we lived in Florida. Bernie and I wanted so much to give that to Willie, but it just wasn't possible. Instead, while we were there, he climbed up on the stalls to pat the other horses and helped the therapists carry gear and get Dani ready to ride. He never once whined about it.

In Tennessee, we couldn't recreate the life we had in Florida. Not the pool, not the dock and the manatees, not the beach, the neighbors, or the bike rides. Bernie and I knew we would have to create a new life from what we had to work with. Dani and Willie were just going to have to become country kids.

One of the first things we did when we moved back was sign Willie up for 4-H Club. It was a special activity he could do that was his own. Either Bernie or I took him to meetings, while the other stayed home with Dani so that Willie could have some time to himself.

He immediately took to the agricultural lifestyle, probably because it had so much to do with animals. Even as we settled into the Gilbert Valley house, we knew it wouldn't be permanent. Our dream was to purchase some acreage farther out in the country and build. I suggested to Bernie that we ease into the farm life while we were still on Gilbert Valley Road. Because it was too late to plant a summer garden, and we didn't have the pasture or a barn for a horse or a coop for chickens, I proposed that we get a couple of goats. Bernie raised his "what-are-you-crazy" eyebrow at me and asked where I thought we should keep them. "Don't you raise that eyebrow at me, Bernie! There's plenty of fenced grass in the back, and they can sleep in the garage." The eyebrow went higher. "My garage? You want to make my workshop into a goat barn?" I pointed out that it was big enough to share and that I bet that Dani would love having goats to pat. End of discussion. I tried not to pull out the "Dani would love . . . " card too often, but it was always effective.

The Wilson County Fair—the biggest in the state—was just a week away. It's about as good as it gets if you're interested in agriculture, farm animals, and machinery, not to mention funnel cakes, cotton candy, Ferris wheels, and merry-go-rounds.

The fair had a big goat barn, and I just knew that when Bernie saw the goats—all prettied up for the fair—he would fall so in love that getting some would become his idea.

We found out that the fair designates a morning for special needs kids on the midway. It's not easy to take full-grown teenagers with no muscle control out of wheelchairs and situate them safely in a ride. Experience has shown us that not everyone has patience when it comes to the physically or mentally disabled, who are not as mobile or agile as they are, so the Special Needs Day was a great opportunity for families with those members.

It can also be disconcerting to be in a crowd of three hundred people, and more than half of them are in a wheelchair; are unable to speak, see, or hear; or can't control their limbs. I was struck again by how truly lucky we were and how minor Dani's limitations seemed sometimes, in comparison to others'.

Bernie was thrilled to get a free pass to be a ten-year-old, and Willie was just beside himself with excitement. For once, having a special needs sister was going to pay off! I am not a big amusement ride person and was more than happy to fill the role of the parent standing on the sidelines, waving each time they came into my view. Dani seemed skeptical at first, but when she climbed into one of those old-timey Model T's with Willie at the wheel, it put a smile on her face that didn't come off the rest of the morning.

Bernie went with her on the faster rides or the ones that went higher in the air, but she wasn't afraid of anything. To her, it was just a bigger, louder, more colorful version of the playgrounds she loved, and for the first time since we left Florida, she had the unrestrained joy on her face that we had not seen in months.

Right before the midway opened to the general population, we headed toward the agricultural side of the fair, my favorite part. I loved everything about it—the blue-ribbon pies, jams, and hams; the animal barns; the quilting exhibit; the educational exhibits of historic rural living. Bernie and Willie were hypnotized by the shiny new farm equipment, from tractors to combines. The Wilson County Fair was better than Disney World to us.

Almost as soon as we walked into the exhibit hall with the food competition, we had to do a 180 and walk back out. Dani thought that all of those cakes, pies, and cookies were for her, and as her last teacher at Spring Creek Elementary in Florida pointed out in a note home, she is fast. I barely got between her hand and a gorgeous coconut cake, and that was the end of the blue-ribbon baked goods portion of our outing to the Wilson County Fair. On the way to the animal barns, we stopped for lunch and got Dani her first corn dog. It struck me that if I could just figure out a way to put all of her food on a stick, we'd have it made at mealtimes.

As delighted as Dani was on the rides, it was the animals—especially the goats and the sheep—that seemed to bring her an inner peace, a calmness and a contentment I had not seen before.

As we went up and down the aisles, watching the farm kids tend these animals that they had raised since birth, Dani was spellbound. We stopped at a few stalls and asked if she could pet them. She giggled at the feel of the sheep's coat and laughed when a goat nibbled at her shorts. I didn't even have to look at Bernie to know that he would soon be sharing his workshop with goats.

Chickens are Bernie's peculiar fascination, and the breeds of fowl at the Wilson County Fair are astounding. He picked Dani up to look at the particularly unusual ones, such as the Polish chickens with their gaudy plumes of head feathers.

The pigs didn't much interest any of us, and Dani seemed a bit taken aback by the cows. It was getting late in the day, but we had promised Willie that we'd check out the tractor display. Dani thought they were just giant versions of Willie's little red jeep, and every time Willie got behind the wheel of one, she clambered up on the passenger side and waited for him to go. "Go!" she commanded. She couldn't understand why Willie wouldn't go and was getting frustrated, so I told Bernie I'd take her to the restroom one more time, then we'd leave. He told me that he and Willie would walk over to the entrance where we had come in and would wait for us.

Dani was dragging, and I had to pick her up to carry her, which was not easy because she was close to seventy pounds. It was like lugging a huge sack of feed. When she saw Bernie and Willie and the strange thing they were holding—a huge cone of blue cotton candy and a similar one of pink cotton candy—she wiggled down and ran to them. She didn't know what it was, but she knew right away which one was for her. She thrust both hands into the middle of the pink cloud before Bernie could react. When she pulled her hand out, it was covered in the spun sugar, and she put all four fingers into her mouth. Bernie, Willie, and I couldn't help it, we laughed out loud, thinking that she was going to get stuck in there. Then she reached the hand still swathed in cotton candy up to brush

Dani's first cotton candy.

hair off her face, with the expected results. She wiped her hands on her shirt, then stuck them back into the cone of pink fluff.

She was covered head to toe in cotton candy and loving it, especially the part she managed to get into her mouth. There wasn't any point in cleaning her up until it was gone, but when it was, we found the nearest spigot and hosed her down.

Despite the sugar overload, both of the kids crashed in the backseat. It had really been a perfect day, and for the first time I was feeling optimistic about being back in Tennessee. I mentally calculated how many goats our backyard would accommodate and how to block off their side of the garage from Bernie's side.

At home I peeled off Dani's sticky, greasy, mustard-stained, dusty shirt and shorts, turned on the water, and steered her under the showerhead, where she stood in a daze, the bottom of the tub turning pale brown from the grime that washed off her legs and arms. I handed her the towel, and she made some half-hearted swipes before I realized that she was just too tired to do it herself.

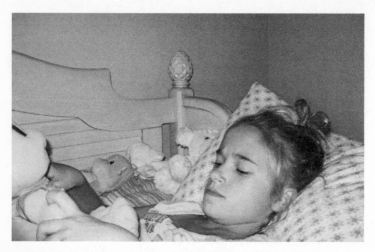

In her bedroom in Tennessee, the first house on Gilbert Valley Road.

I wrapped the towel around her, along with a tight squeeze, then took her to her room. I helped her on with her pajamas and tucked her Hello Kitty comforter around her. I found Lullaby Gloworm on the floor under her bed, but Dani was already asleep by the time I laid it in her arms.

25

Home

During the long school break that started the week before Christmas and didn't end until an eternity later, the first week of January, I was reminded of why I had hated winters so much in Tennessee. They were relentlessly, interminably dreary—cold, wet, and gray. We didn't get the beautiful snowstorms that I had grown up with in Michigan that laid a fluffy white blanket over our world, making everything still and quiet and primed for sledding, snowball fights from behind snow forts, snow men, and snow angels.

Winter precipitation in the Cumberland Valley region where we lived was drizzle, rain, sleet, or ice. And because we were in a valley, all of that nastiness lingered on and on. It rarely snowed, and when it did, it was barely enough for a snowman or sledding but just enough to send everyone racing to the grocery store in a panic. If there was an ice storm—which was more frequent—you could count on schools to be closed until the last patch of asphalt in Wilson County was clear. Skies were clouded over for days on end. The cold was a damp cold, and once it got in your bones it settled there, no matter how hot a bath you drew. But it never got cold enough to freeze over a pond for ice-skating. I had spent many winter days skating when I was a kid, gliding free around the outdoor rink until my toes were close to frozen and my mother sent my dad looking for me to come home for dinner.

Most of the time, from November through February, the dismal weather kept everyone inside. After more than five years of living in Florida, we were used to being outdoors all of the time, so being cooped up in the small house on Gilbert Valley Road made us a little cranky and stir crazy.

I had gotten my goats, though—boys Salem and Derby and girls Precious and Peaches. They gave us a reason to get out and stomp around; feeding, grooming, and chasing them around the yard was entertainment for us. When Bernie was working on something in his workshop—which was all of the time—he turned on the big industrial heater, and we all went out to keep him and the goats company. Willie helped Bernie, just as Bernie had done with his dad. I think it made Bernie feel better as he grieved for his father, who had passed away in November. Dani pestered the goats, especially Peaches, her favorite. We got a Pyrenees puppy we named Chances—as in second chances—which gave Dani another warm and fuzzy animal to love and Willie a project. One of the twice-weekly 4-H meetings he went to was a dog obedience class that he and Chances were enrolled in together. I considered sending Dani along for some obedience training, but I didn't think they would get the joke.

She was on the waiting list for an opening with the therapeutic horseback-riding farm that was nearby. On Wednesdays after school, she had private speech and occupational therapy. We had a busy schedule, but we were still getting on one another's nerves. I was looking forward to when the frost danger passed, and we could plant a garden. That would give all of us something else to do together outside.

Our real estate agent continued to send us listings of farm properties, but nothing was in our price range, which was pretty limited after our last year in Florida. On February 14, we got an e-mail from the agent with the subject line "Happy Valentine's Day!" I thought that was sweet, but when I opened it, she continued with a note saying she thought she had found "a place you will LOVE!" What she left out was the word "only": a place that only you two crazy people will love!

So on that dreary, damp, cold, gray Tennessee winter day in February, the four of us were in Bernie's truck following her car down a winding road to the very farthest edge of Wilson County. I knew we had told her we wanted to be out in the country, but we had already gone nearly four miles from the interstate, and all we had seen along the side of this narrow winding road was a little house or a mobile home every tenth or so of a mile, two churches, one cemetery, several barns, many cows, a few horses, and one home business that doubled as a beauty parlor and a tanning salon. I was getting a little nauseated from going up and down the hills, and Dani was starting to rock in the backseat.

Finally, the real estate agent slowed down. On the left was a beautiful white wooden antebellum home with wide porches that ran the length of the first and second floors, tall windows framed by green shutters on both levels, and graceful supporting columns and brick chimneys jutting out of the roof. I could see a small yellow clapboard guesthouse behind the main house and a sizable herd of goats in a large wood-fenced pen. Even on the gloom of this ugly winter day, it was heavenly. I felt like Scarlett O'Hara coming home, and if it had been a movie, the soundtrack to *Gone with the Wind* would have magically swelled from the car radio.

To my dismay, the real estate agent didn't turn into that drive but continued another twenty-five feet down the road before coming to a stop at a metal gate on the right. I hoped that we were turning around and going back to Tara, but instead she got out of the car to open the gate, then yelled back for us to shut it behind us.

The rutted gravel path went down a slight incline, then back up, and there, just beyond the shoulder-high grass on what had been the front lawn was the house, though not so much a house as a ruin. I reluctantly got out of the car, thinking she must have mistaken us for certifiably crazy people, rather than just run-of-the-mill crazy people. Bernie, on the other hand, was out and bounding up the crumbling stairs.

The agent chattered away, telling us that the "charming Arts and Crafts bungalow was built in 1923." It looked like it hadn't had any maintenance since about 1923. In some parts the roof was caving in, except for over the porch, where it just sagged. The chimneys were missing large portions of their bricks, several of the eaves that ran from the sides of the house to under the roof were rotting, most of the glass in the windows was broken, and the front door hung crookedly. The stone steps leading up to the porch were cracked and separating from the landing. There was no color anywhere—the sky was gray, the grass was brown, the house was a dingy white, and even the two large barns that we could see in the field behind the house, once painted green, had completely faded and were in a similar state of disrepair.

The realtor tugged hard on the listing front door and cheerfully called for us to come inside. I was sure that a veritable terrarium of spiders, snakes, and rodents awaited us.

The power had long since been shut off, so it was freezing inside and we couldn't turn on any lights, but even in the gloomy natural light we could see that it had once been a beautiful home. The front room had the artisan built-in cabinetry that Arts and Crafts homes are known for, and I could see Bernie looking it over with a gleam in his eye. Against one wall was a huge stone fireplace, and on the wall next to that, French doors leading to what I supposed was once the dining room. A long hall led down one side of the house, past three large rooms on the left, and then a wide staircase rose to the second floor. The wood floors were a disaster, as were the plaster walls. There had obviously been many leaks from the roof, and water stains discolored the high ceilings. There was trash and debris all over the place, as well as pigeon droppings from where the birds had flown through broken windows.

We went cautiously up the stairs and found more of the same mess. While I stood aghast at the doorway of the so-called bathroom, which had no tub or shower and a sorry-looking commode and sink, Bernie had gone to the room at the far end of the hall. Dani was sitting on his shoulders, and they were looking out the four windows on the front of the house. I stepped gingerly across the floor strewn with piles of dried leaves, sticks, and what looked like animal bones to see what had captured their attention.

Spread before us, as far as the eye could see, were rolling hills of pasture dotted with red barns, tall old trees with gigantic trunks and massive gnarled limbs, fallow fields awaiting spring planting, and little white dots of farmhouses. It was winter-drab, but within a month or so the pastures would be washed in pale green; oaks and hackberries would pop buds; Bradford pear and dogwood trees would erupt in pretty white blossoms; red buds would be in the pink; and tiny seedlings would push through the dirt in the fields. In that moment, I was reminded of all that I loved about spring in Tennessee and how much I had missed the changing of the seasons when we lived in Florida. These tired old windows with their dirty, broken glass panes would frame a glorious landscape of resurrection and renewal, of life bursting forth from a place that had seemed barren and dead. I could see it in my mind's eye as surely as if it was right in front of me.

Willie came in to join the party, a big "Wow!" his succinct reaction to the panoramic view of bucolic bounty before us. Bernie took my hand and squeezed it. "Diane." Oh, I knew Bernie, and I knew what was coming. He was about to turn my words about Dani from that very first photo of her—lost, empty, and hopeless—right around on me.

"Diane. This house needs us. This land needs us. And Willie and Dani need this place. Our family needs this place."

And so, because the bank that owned it and wanted it off their hands offered us a price that seemed to verify that it was meant to be, we bought it. Twenty-six acres, five outbuildings, and one very needy 1923 Arts and Crafts bungalow. With no kitchen.

Because certain jobs were outside our area of expertise, we had to hire contractors to rewire the whole house, install central heat and air, and put on a new roof. While they were doing that and the kids were in school, Bernie and I hauled out trash, filling an endless caravan of dumpsters that were dropped off empty in our yard, then hauled away. The man across the road offered to bush-hog the yard, which we gratefully accepted. I told him that as soon as I had a kitchen, I would bake him a cake.

When the weather began to warm, and the house was safe for the kids to be in it, we brought the big enclosed trampoline and the wooden play set over from the Gilbert Valley house. We put the play set behind the back side of the house and the trampoline out front so that we could keep an eye on Dani from whichever part of the house we were working on. Willie looked at the new place as twenty-six acres of unexplored territory and happily roamed the property with his metal detector and a canvas sack for storing the treasures he unearthed. Some afternoons we let him go off on his own so he could have some Willie time, and other times he took Dani along as his "helper."

Precious and Peaches had babies, and we kept them in the garage at the old house because we didn't have a secured field for them yet, but we brought Salem and Derby over to one of the barns. Because the kids would be zoned for a new school once we moved, we stayed in the Gilbert Valley house until the end of the term, and while we made the farmhouse livable.

A small life insurance policy from Bernie's dad helped out a lot with what we had to purchase, but we did all of the work ourselves: all of the walls were dry-walled and painted; all of the floors refinished; the bathrooms tiled and the sinks, the tubs, the showers, and the new commodes installed; the windows replaced; and the steps repaired.

As the "charming" Arts and Crafts bungalow emerged like a butterfly from its cocoon, so did both of our children begin to metamorphose into the next phases of their lives. Willie was becoming more self-confident and independent, while at the same time assuming more responsibility for Dani, especially as Bernie and I had been so consumed with the work on the house.

Willie's baby face was beginning to shed its round softness, and I could see the young man who would walk into my kitchen fully grown some morning soon. He even asked that we stop calling him Willie, because "it sounds like a little boy's name." He wanted to be called William, and although I said, "Sure," I turned my head so that he wouldn't see the tears in my eyes. I was proud of him but felt a pang of wistfulness for my baby boy who was disappearing day by day.

Dani was settling happily into our new home, and I think maybe it was because she had been a part of it since the start. She had picked out her room the very first day we were there as if her name was painted over the door. When we finally moved the furniture over from Gilbert Valley, we placed her bed so that when she woke up and opened her eyes, she would be looking out those windows, now repaired and sparkly clean.

We eventually brought all of the animals over—Precious and Peaches and their babies, the annoying talking, biting parrot, the Pomeranians, and Chances. A neighbor's Pyrenees had puppies she couldn't keep, so we took in all three of them—all girls—to give Chances some playmates.

The day we finished the kitchen, we celebrated with the first home-cooked meal we had eaten in months. Even cleaning up didn't feel like a chore when I looked out the window over the sink and saw Chances loping through the greening pasture, trailed by Shy-Anne, Dori, and Spicy, her adoring little sisters.

Dani helped me plant a kitchen garden out back, and when it needed watering, she could hold the hose, although she was easily distracted by any of the animals that roamed around the yard and the fenced fields. Our quartet of goats had expanded to a full-blown choir of more than two dozen, and it seemed like half of them were expecting as well.

Bernie's mail order of baby chicks was delivered in late March to William and Dani's delight. There's nothing like opening a big box and finding a hundred adorable balls of fuzz inside to make a kid happy. Dani loved to reach inside the box and gently cup one of them in her hands, then put it down and get another. The future egg layers were still in the mud room under warming lights while we turned one of the shacks into a coop and until they were big enough to fend off the dogs, and I took a secret delight in how their incessant peeping had to annoy the parrot.

On the day that I went back to the empty Gilbert Valley house to give it one final cleaning before putting it on the market, I passed by a little dog lying on the side of the road. I figured he had been hit by a car and left for dead. His white coat was stained with fresh and dried blood, and he yelped when I picked him up, but he let me place him on a blanket in the backseat of the car. I took him to the shelter first, but when the shelter workers told me they would put him down because his injuries were so severe, what could I do but take him to our own vet to be patched up? He recuperated in the laundry room until he could limp around on his own. William named him Frosty, and he was the only one of all of our dogs who was allowed access inside and out through a doggie door Bernie installed for him near the back door.

There was always some fixing or project that needed tending to. Though the neglected and abandoned house was becoming a loved and cared-for home, it was and probably always will be a work in progress. The folks at our nearby Lowe's know us by name, and the floor guys and gals always have a couple of lollipops in their work aprons for Dani and William.

At the end of the first summer that we were in the farmhouse, we went to get some lumber Bernie needed to build another nursery pen in the barn, where the rapidly growing herd of goats resided. I was pestering him to see if Lowe's might be having an end-of-season sale on above-ground pools. I knew it wouldn't be the same as our Florida pool, but it would give William and Dani something to look forward to next spring.

Dani held her arms up to Bernie to be put in the cargo section of the cart, and, of course, even though at her size she looked a bit ridiculous sitting there, Bernie complied. Whatever his little girl wants, she gets. William and I walked along behind them. He was wearing me out about a miniature horse he had seen an ad for somewhere. "William Christian Lierow! The last thing we need is a horse on top of everything else!" "But Mom! It's a miniature horse!" "William! Horses have giant appetites! Even miniature ones. And winter is coming, so it won't be able to graze and will need feed. Feed is not free!" "I'll take care of it, Mom! I promise. If you let me get a couple of rabbits, I can raise them to sell to make money for the feed. You know how much Dani would love to have a miniature horse, right?" Wow. My own son had resorted to playing the "you know how much Dani . . ." card. "And Mom, guess what else? Her name is Hope!"

We practically rear-ended Bernie, who had stopped in the middle of the aisle. He gestured toward Dani sitting cross-legged in the cart. She was looking at Bernie, directly into his eyes, saying something quietly over and over. William and I stopped our bickering to listen.

"I pity . . . I pity . . . I pity . . ." Pity? Had she overheard someone saying something about pity? About pitying her?

A school photo of Dani that Diane thinks
was taken in the fall of 2008.

Bernie gently urged her to say it again. "What are you saying,
sweetheart? Tell us again."

We all leaned in closer to her. "I pity." Bernie was puzzled. "You
pity? Dani pity? I pity?"

Dani smiled at the three of us—her father, her mother, and her
sweet big brother—and patting herself on the chest, she said,
"I pretty."

On an ordinary afternoon in the lumber department of the
Lowe's store in Lebanon, an extraordinary thing had happened.
While her family erupted with shouts of joy, a little girl with the
face of an angel and the unwavering faith of a survivor patted her
heart and said as clear as day, "I pretty."

Epilogue

Bernie and I are pretty simple people, leading pretty ordinary lives. Like millions of other people around the world, we work, we parent, we try to be good partners to each other. We do all we can to make sure our kids mind their manners, do their homework, eat healthy food, get fresh air, respect others, make good decisions, have compassionate hearts, and say their prayers before bed. We don't care so much whether they are "gifted" as we do that they are kind, generous, and thoughtful. To us, that *is* gifted.

On the rare occasions that we go out, we go out as a family, but we prefer to be at home. We find camaraderie and support in our church and with our close friends.

We do not by any measure seek the spotlight. We adopted Dani because we were called to do it and because we fell in love with her before we even met her. We feel blessed every single day that we were led to her and that we were able to overcome all of the obstacles so she could become our daughter.

The attention we received as a result of the newspaper article and then appearing on *Oprah* overwhelmed us. Not just the enormousness of the response, but that people felt we had done something special, something remarkable. That we were heroes, as many people said.

We only did what thousands of other people in America do again and again—we brought a child into our home whom we did not conceive, but who was as much a member of our family as if we had. We are no more special than all of those others who do the same.

But Dani's story is compelling, and Dani haunts the people who meet her in a way that is hard to understand unless you have met her yourself. As uncomfortable as it was for us to open our home to a newspaper reporter and a photographer, to create a website, to sit onstage with Oprah Winfrey, and, finally, to write this book, we did it for two reasons.

First, we hope that by reading our story, people may be inspired to look into adoption, foster care, or volunteering for whatever the guardian ad litem program may be in your state. In our area, it is CASA—Court Appointed Special Advocate. These volunteers give abused, neglected, and abandoned children a voice and an advocate, often the first and only advocate they have ever had.

Second, we felt that if we told Dani's story, and it inspired people to call their local adoption agencies, meet some of the children who were looking for their forever families, and take a leap of faith, then what Dani suffered in the nearly seven years of being confined in an unimaginable hell will not have been in vain. Even if reading her story causes just one of you to be brave enough to make that call when you know something is not right in the house next door, with the little girl at your daughter's bus stop, or with the little boy in your son's day care, then it was worth it.

If we had not told Dani's story, then all of her suffering, all of her struggles, and all of the strength she somehow found to survive would have been for nothing. If telling her story helps other children in the foster care system find a home, then her ordeal may be the catalyst for a positive outcome.

When people hear our story and learn about Dani, they all ask the same questions: "What is her prognosis? How far will she go? Will she ever learn to speak?"

And we have the same answer every time: "We don't know." Incredibly, there are many children who are neglected as badly as Dani was, but it is extremely rare that one goes undiscovered and lives as long in such an abominable situation. Certainly, as Dr. Armstrong pointed out to us, doctors and scientists can't experiment on children as they do on animals. So there is really no way of knowing for sure, although research has painted a pretty grim picture.

We know that about 80 percent of the brain is developed by a child's fifth birthday, and that the critical years for language development are between two and three years of age. Some senses are much better developed when we are born than others. Hearing, for example, is pretty close to perfect at birth. Vision is much less developed in newborns, and it requires many things coming together for a child to develop visual skills.

Your brain is born with all of the neurons you are ever going to have, and what happens in the process of development is that you build connections—synapses—with the neurons, or you shed the neurons. It is known as pruning, like pruning a tree. Those things that aren't used, you lose. Those that you use, you build and develop more and more connections.

Babies are born hard-wired to learn, but it takes relationships, stimulation, and a healthy environment to do that. Dani was born with all of the neurons she was ever going to have, hard-wired to learn. The heartbreaking tragedy is that no one in her life provided her with the relationships, the stimulation, and the environment that were necessary to build the connections she needed to realize her potential, whatever that was. So many of those neurons she was born with were lost. Forever? Science says so.

Some forms of mental retardation are genetic: Down syndrome for one; Fragile X, for another. Genetic testing that was done on

Dani when she was taken into custody showed none of those genes. Fetal alcohol exposure can also cause mental retardation, but her birth mother claims that she did not drink during her pregnancy. Dani was never diagnosed with autism.

Dr. Kathleen Armstrong tested Dani three times. She said that in thirty years of practice as a psychologist, she had never seen a child of Dani's age so severely neglected. It was her opinion that had Dani been removed from the home when she was three or four, when calls were first made to the DCF, the prognosis for her could have been different.

Reports written by Dr. Bruce Perry state that the earlier and more pervasive the neglect, the more devastating the developmental problems for the child. The earlier that a child is removed from such an environment of severe neglect, the more positive and hopeful the prognosis, although, in reality, the child is unlikely to ever become the adult he or she might have been had the child not been so severely neglected in those crucial developmental years.

Bernie and I know all of that. And we know this: after Dr. Armstrong tested her, the best-case scenario that she envisioned for Dani was that she would end up in a nursing home, institutionalized for the remainder of her life. We know that aside from Garet White, no one in the DCF believed that Dani could be adopted, and, indeed, people discouraged us when we expressed interest.

We know that when we first met Dani in January 2007, she bounced from being a wild child, hitting herself with her fist and screaming animal-like noises, to being a drooling, lethargic, unengaged child with developmental skills that were somewhere between an infant's and a toddler's. There was no telling what state Dani might be in from one moment to the next.

Three years ago, when we brought her home for the first trial visit with us, she wet all the way through her diaper and clothes onto the backseat of the car, and she was completely oblivious to it, as an infant would be.

Just recently after a therapeutic horseback riding session, when Dani dismounted she took off like a shot out of the barn. Bernie ran after her to see where she was going and found her on the seat in the port-a-john, with her pants down around her ankles, her helmet lopsided on her head, and a look of total relief on her face. I had warned him when they left the house that she had drunk three sodas that afternoon at a school party. I can't believe she managed such self-control through a one-hour lesson, but she did it! She loves riding so much that she doesn't want to come off the horse, so she knows she has to do whatever it takes to stay dry. No one would have imagined that for her when she was taken into state custody in 2005.

When she first came to us, she ate so much food—stuffing it into her mouth with her hands—that she literally made herself sick. She didn't know when to stop and was afraid she wouldn't get any more. Now she makes herself a snack and pours herself a drink, and at mealtimes when she is no longer hungry, she stops eating.

When she first came to us, she floated directionless around the pool in a life jacket like a human bobber. Now she swims like a fish, traversing the bottom of the pool, holding her breath from one side to the other, and gliding like a mermaid.

When she first came to us, she did not participate at all in helping us dress or undress her. Now, she at least makes an attempt. This past winter, when the kids were out of school on break, I had the flu. Bernie had a job in Nashville, so I didn't have the luxury of burrowing under the covers until I felt better. Goats, chickens, horses, and dogs don't feed themselves, and it's too big a job for William alone, so one morning after Bernie left, I hauled myself out of bed for the chores. Dani was still asleep in her room. When I came back into the house, she was downstairs, fully dressed. I called Bernie on his cell phone to ask him why he had put her to bed with her clothes on the night before. He assured me that he had done no such thing, and when I went upstairs to investigate, I found her pajamas and the pull-ups she sometimes still wears at night on the floor in the bathroom. She had taken everything off, gone to the bathroom, picked the clothes up from the floor in her bedroom where Bernie had left them, and put them on herself.

When she first came to us, she didn't know what a book was or what it was for. Now, when she sees me sitting on the sofa, looking as if I have nothing to do, she brings a book or five for me to read to her while she curls up beside me.

She is a very busy girl. She can turn on the little organ in the playroom, and she likes to press the keys or sit on them, to make spooky noises. She can take everything out of the refrigerator in less than twenty minutes or as long as it takes me to shower upstairs. One day, she took all of the cups out of the cupboard, filled each of them with water, and lined them all up on the counter.

She knows right from wrong. She knows when she is doing something she is not supposed to do or has something she is not supposed to have. She loves to play little tricks on us, and she has a sense of humor.

We know she's taking it all in. We know that it takes longer and is a more complicated route for something to get from the outside to the inside and out again, but she gets it. She has a hard time getting it out, but we believe she understands.

What is her prognosis? How far will she go? Will she ever learn to speak?

We don't know. But back when we first had Dani with us in Fort Myers Beach, I was reminded in a very humbling way that not knowing isn't the worst thing. When she started at Spring Creek Elementary, she was placed in the lowest-level classroom. We were fighting the school to have her moved out of that room and up to the next level.

One day I went to pick her up her from school, and the mother of a severely mentally and physically disabled young boy in that classroom smiled at me as she wheeled him toward the door.

She remarked on how pretty and sweet Dani was and then said, "You're so lucky. It may not seem that way to you right now, but you are. You have no idea how much Danielle might accomplish. I know my son will never get any better than this. But Danielle has so much potential and so many possibilities."

She was right, of course. I like to remember a conversation Bernie had with Mr. O'Keefe; I think it was after *Oprah*. He told Bernie that he wasn't surprised that Dani has progressed as far as she has. "Sometimes people assume a lack of intelligence when there is a handicap. But I would assume there is some type of intelligence there. When I saw her pick up the skill of walking up the stairs so quickly, that made me think there was more there than appeared to the eye."

And then this man who has cared for some of the most hopeless children I have ever seen told Bernie, "I try to remain an optimist. I've heard about miracles, I've seen miracles happen. I believe miracles can happen. I have hope and I have faith, and you and Diane do, too. Don't ever become hopeless. Don't doubt your faith."

We can't answer that question of how far Dani might go, not only because we don't know, but because it doesn't really matter to us. She is our daughter, she is William's little sister, and we love her as much when she is having a meltdown, caroming around the house and crying, "Woo woo woo woo" as we do when she looks in our eyes, pats her heart, and says, "I good."

To us, every milestone Dani reaches is a little miracle. Every day is a walk in hope, faith, and gratitude.

We ended up trading some goats for that miniature horse William was needling me about. Her name is Hope. Naturally, feeling as if she needed some companions of her own breed, we got two more miniature horses to keep her company, Izzy and Oreo.

But Hope is definitely Dani's horse. Dani loves to walk beside her, pat her, and lay across her back, but Hope is a bit too small for Dani to ride. Besides, not long after we got her, we discovered that

Empower Me Day Camp, summer 2010
water play.

Hope wasn't fat, as we had first thought: she was pregnant. In the first days of spring 2010, as the earth around us was awakening to life again, we gathered in the barn with the bleating goats and watched in wonder as Hope gave birth to a tiny foal. We laughed (and I cried) as she struggled to her feet on her wobbly spindly legs, and we welcomed her to our crazy world.

We named her Joy.

Acknowledgments

Diane and Bernie Lierow and Kay West would like to thank the team who guided this book to fruition: Sarah Lazin and Manuela Jessel at Sarah Lazin Books; Stephen Power, Richard DeLorenzo, and Ellen Wright at Wiley; and Robert K. Oermann for playing matchmaker.

Our sincere gratitude to Dani's first angels, most especially Garet White for going above and beyond; Plant City Police Detective Mark Holste; Kevin O'Keefe and Marisa Perez of Sanders Memorial Elementary; and Casey Foote and Leslie Goldenberg of The School District of Lee County. Thanks to the Heart Gallery and to Carolyn Eastman of Children's Board of Hillsborough County; to Lane DeGregory and Melissa Lyttle of the *St. Petersburg Times*; and to everyone at *Oprah*, especially producer Staci Strazis, and Oprah Winfrey for her kindness.

Diane and Bernie Lierow wish to thank all the wonderful volunteers at Naples Equestrian Challenge, STARRS, and Empower Me Day Camp; our dear friends in Fort Myers Beach: Dorothy and Paul LaPiccola and Doris and Bill Kenny, and Mike and Evie Barnes, for allowing Diane to have such a flexible work schedule when we first got Danielle; our children Paul and Steven Willhite, and Shawn and Ryan Lierow; Rachell Willhite; and everyone who has touched Danielle's life along her journey.

Kay West thanks the Lierows for their trust and friendship; my children Joy and Harry West, for their patience, understanding, support, and love; my family for their encouragement; and my army of friends for their humor, cheerleading, and reprieves of wine and whine. Much gratitude to Sarah Lazin, for talking me off the ledge more than once.

To follow Dani's progress: http://www.danisstory.org/

If you suspect a child is being abused, the National Hotline is: http://www.thechildabusehotline.com/

For more information on fostering, adoption, and the Heart Gallery: http://www.heartgalleryofamerica.org/